Firefighter Tests

www.How2Become.com

Orders: Please contact www.How2Become.com

You can also order via the e mail address info@how2become.com

ISBN: 9781907558122

First published 2010

Second Edition, Updated in 2017.

Copyright © 2017 How2Become Ltd.

Typeset for How2Become Ltd by Gemma Butler

Disclaimer

Every effort has been made to ensure that the information contained within this guide is accurate at the time of publication. How2Become Ltd is not responsible for anyone failing any part of any selection process as a result of the information contained within this guide. How2Become Ltd and their authors cannot accept any responsibility for any errors or omissions within this guide, however caused. No responsibility for loss or damage occasioned by any person acting, or refraining from action, as a result of the material in this publication can be accepted by How2Become Ltd.

The information within this guide does not represent the views of any third-party service or organisation.

Contents

Welcome

Dear Sir/Madam,

Welcome to your new guide – 'Firefighter Tests'. This guide has been designed to help you prepare for the written test element of the national firefighter selection process.

The author of this guide, Richard McMunn, spent over 16 years in the UK Fire Service. He worked at many different fire stations at every position up to Station Manager, and he has also sat on numerous interview panels assessing potential candidates to join the job.

You will find his advice invaluable and inspiring in your pursuit to joining what is probably one of the most exciting careers available. Whilst the selection process to join the Fire Service is highly competitive, there are a number of things you can do in order to improve your chances of success, and they are all contained within this guide.

The guide itself has been split up into useful sections to make it easier for you to prepare for each element of the testing process. Read each section carefully before trying out the different test questions that have been provided by the author. Don't ever give up on your dreams; if you really want to become a firefighter, then you can do it.

The guide will focus primarily on the firefighter tests that form part of the national firefighter selection process in the UK. If you need any help with other elements of the selection process, then we offer a wide range of products to assist you, including application form completion, interview DVD's and even a 1-day firefighter training course. These are all available through our online shop:

www.How2Become.com.

Once again, thank you for your purchasing this guide and we wish you every success in your pursuit to becoming a firefighter.

Work hard, stay focused and secure your dream career…

Good luck and best wishes,

The how2become team

Preface by Author Richard McMunn

I joined the Fire Service on the 25th of January 1993 after completing four years in the Fleet Air Arm branch of the Royal Navy. In the build up to joining the Fire Service I embarked on a comprehensive training programme that would see me pass the selection process with relative ease. The reason why I passed the selection process with ease was solely due to the amount of preparation and hard work that I had put in during the build-up.

Yes I admit, the written tests were different back then, but the process was still the same. When I sat the firefighter tests back in 1992, you had to be competent with numbers, good with the English language, and also possess an ability to interpret mechanical concepts and patterns. It also helped if you were from a military background.

In 2017, you must be competent at different things, and that is what I will concentrate on during the content of this guide.

So, what qualifies me to help you to pass the firefighter written tests? Well, apart from serving nearly 17 years in the job, I was also heavily involved in firefighter recruitment and training. I have administered the firefighter tests, marked application forms, sat on interview panels and even been an instructor on four firefighter recruit training courses.

Therefore, the knowledge and test questions that I will provide you with, will go a long way to assisting you during your preparation. I do not claim, however, that the questions provided within this guide will be identical to the ones that you will undertake. That would be wrong, and it would not help you to develop the right skills and qualities that are required to become a firefighter.

The purpose of this guide, apart from providing you with a host of sample test questions, is to help you to understand why the Fire Service asks you the questions that they do. If you understand why they ask these types of questions, then your chances of passing the tests will greatly increase.

I have always been a great believer in preparation. Preparation was my key to success, and it is also yours. Without the right level of preparation, you will be setting out on the route to failure. The Fire Service is very hard to join, but if you follow the steps that I have compiled within this guide then you will increase your chances of passing the written test element of selection dramatically. Remember, you are learning how to be a successful candidate, not a successful firefighter. That will come later.

I make no excuses for stating that, in order to prepare effectively for the firefighter written tests, you must learn and understand thoroughly the personal qualities and attributes (PQAs) that are relevant to the role of a firefighter. This is simply because many of the questions you are likely to face are based around the PQAs. If you know the PQAs inside out, then the answers to the questions will be easier to identify – in some cases they will even jump out at you!

In addition to learning the PQAs, I also recommend that you become proficient in the use of basic numerical arithmetic. Firefighters need to be competent in the use of numbers, including addition, subtraction, multiplication, and division. After all, your life – and those of others – could one day become dependent on your ability to carry out simple basic numerical calculations whilst under pressure.

So, let's get started and take a look at the different types of tests that the Fire Service uses in order to assess firefighter applicants.

Best wishes,

Richard McMunn

Chapter 1
About the Firefighter
Written Tests

No matter which Fire and Rescue Service you want to join the UK, you'll need to pass several written ability tests to get recruited. These tests are designed to assess your cognitive skills in several areas, and allow recruiters to evaluate how suitable you are for the non-physical side of the role.

As a firefighter, you need to be able to make correct decisions under serious time constraints, and make use of many skills such as mathematical aptitude and situational awareness. As such, recruiters are keen to test these skills during the notoriously tough recruitment process.

Most services do so using the National Firefighter Ability (NFA) Tests, which consist of the following: the Working with Numbers Test, the Understanding Information Test, the Situational Awareness and Problem Solving Test, and the National Firefighter Questionnaire.

The NFA Tests you'll face will usually consist of multiple-choice questions. The assessments themselves will normally be carried out at a local test centre or Fire Service establishment, and will take approximately three hours to complete. You will receive full details about the tests prior to the test day.

But, you need to be aware that some Fire and Rescue Services incorporate other ability tests – such as verbal reasoning and mechanical reasoning tests – into their processes. So, before you go any further, you should check the website of the service you intend to apply for. There, you will be able to find out which tests you will actually need to prepare for, and then turn to the relevant sections of this book to get practising!

Here is a list of all the tests you may face during a firefighter selection process, depending on the service you apply to:

- **The Working with Numbers Test;**
- **The Understanding Information Test;**
- **The Situational Awareness and Problem Solving Test;**
- **The National Firefighter Questionnaire;**
- **Verbal Reasoning Tests;**
- **Mechanical Reasoning Tests.**

This questionnaire has been designed so as to provide information on your style and your behaviour. The Fire Service will use this information, along with the other results of your tests, to determine whether or not you are suitable to become a firefighter. We have found over the years that many people struggle with this part of the test. The questions often repeat themselves throughout the questionnaire, albeit in a slightly different manner. One of the most effective ways to understand this type of test is to fully learn the PQAs. If you know them, then you will fully understand the style and behaviour that the Fire Service is looking for from successful applicants; more on this later.

Before we take a look at a number of different sample test questions, let us explore in greater detail why fire services are assessing you by using ability tests and a questionnaire. Understanding why they are assessing you in this manner will serve to help you pass the tests.

To start, think about the following two questions:

1. *Why is the Fire Service assessing me in these areas?*

2. *What would they expect to see from successful candidates?*

Now, let's look at some potential answers to these questions.

I. The Fire Service want to be sure that I am capable of working with numbers in a fast and competent manner, because this is what firefighters are required to do as part of their role. They must use calculations effectively, especially when using breathing apparatus and operating the pump on a fire engine. Whilst I don't need to be a mathematics professor, I do need to be capable of working out simple arithmetic calculations in an accurate and speedy manner. Therefore, I will make sure that I practice plenty of sample numerical questions in the build up to the tests.

The Fire Service also wants to be sure that I can understand information that is relevant to the role of a firefighter. This will demonstrate to the assessors that I have the potential to pass the firefighter training course and that I also have the ability to complete any future professional development programmes during my career. During the ability testing I will be asked questions that determine my understanding and awareness of situations that I could be faced with whilst serving as a firefighter. Therefore, in order to successfully pass the tests, I will need to fully learn and understand the PQAS that are relevant to the role. If I learn and understand these, I will be far better prepared than the majority of other applicants.

Finally, the Fire service wants to be sure that I am aware of situations relevant to the role of a firefighter, and that I can apply a common-sense attitude and a safe approach to those situations.

2. The Fire service would expect to see accurate calculations whilst I am working with numbers and that I can follow appropriate guidance that is provided during the tests. They would expect to see that I am capable of understanding job relevant information and answering questions correctly based around that information.

    They would also want to see me make common sense, safe decisions when presented with specific scenarios. Firefighters no longer take unnecessary risks during fires and operational incidents, and they will certainly not put themselves or other people in un- necessary danger.

Now that we have answers to the questions, let's set out a simple action plan that dictates exactly what you should do to make sure that you match up to all the qualities discussed in these answers. In this particular case it will look something like this:

1. I will embark on a structured development programme that will improve my ability to work with numbers. I will carry out a large number of sample test questions and I will obtain further testing booklets and resources to allow me to do that. If I need further assistance or development in this area, then I will seek the help of a qualified tutor.

2. I will make sure that I fully understand the role of a firefighter so that I can respond to the questions based around 'understanding information'. In order to achieve this, I will read, learn and memorise the Personal Qualities and Attributes that are relevant to the role of a firefighter. By learning and understanding about the role of a firefighter,

especially in relation to the PQAS, I will be able to respond to 'situational awareness questions' more effectively.

Even though the above process is a simple one, it is important that you carry it out as it will focus your mind on the areas that you need to work on and develop. Now let's move on to the different testing areas themselves.

Ability Tests

Within this guide we have provided you with a number of sample test questions to help you prepare for the ability tests. Use the questions provided as a practice aid only. Remember that these will not be the exact questions that you will be required to answer on the day.

Prior to the tests:

- Preparation, preparation, preparation! In the weeks before the test, work hard to improve your skills in the testing areas. In addition to the tests contained within this guide there are numerous other testing resources available at www.How2Become.com. Try out as many test questions as possible and make sure you learn from your mistakes.

- Get a good night's sleep before the test day and don't drink any alcohol or caffeine in the build up to the tests. It is important that you drink plenty or water in order to keep yourself hydrated.

- On the morning of the test, get up early and have a final run through a number of sample test questions, just to get your brain working.

- Eat a good healthy breakfast such as bran flakes and a chopped-up banana. Don't eat anything too heavy that will make you feel bloated or sluggish – remember, you want to be at your best.

- Whilst not essential, we recommend you wear a smart formal outfit for the testing day. The reason for this is simply because the majority of candidates will be casually dressed. It is better to stand out for the right reasons. A member of the testing staff might just be on the interview panel.

- Check the news for any potential traffic problems and leave in good time to arrive at the test centre with plenty of time to spare. Take a small bottle of water with you to help keep you hydrated.

On the Day:

- Arrive in good time at the test location. Make sure you know where the test centre is.

- Ensure that you know exactly what you are required to do - do not be afraid to ask questions if you are unsure.

- Follow the instructions you are given exactly.

- During the tests, try to eliminate as many wrong answers as possible. For example, with numerical tests, a quick estimate may help you to discard several of the options without working out every alternative.

- Work as quickly and accurately as you can. Both speed and accuracy are important, so do not spend too long on any one question.

- Do not waste time on a difficult question. If you are stuck, leave it and move on, but make sure you leave a space on the answer sheet!

- Don't worry if you do not finish all of the questions in the allocated time. If you do, go over your answers again to check for errors.

- Keep your head down and concentrate on the task in hand. It is your job to do as best as you possibly can during the tests, so it is important that you concentrate.

Chapter 2
The NFA Working
with Numbers Test

This multiple-choice test assesses your ability to understand and work with numerical information of a type that a firefighter is likely to experience whilst carrying out his or her role.

The test requires candidates to perform combinations of addition, subtraction, multiplication and division as well as estimations of numerical data. The test usually consists of 32 questions, which must be answered within a set time limit. The questions are usually based around different Fire Service-related scenarios, each with five or six related questions. The scenarios used may cover the following areas:

- Reading gauges at a factory fire;

- Monitoring fuel supplies;

- Using breathing apparatus;

- Managing hoses;

- Injuries and fire deaths in the home;

- Using hoses at a fire.

Take a look at the following sample 'using breathing apparatus' question.

Using Breathing Apparatus

Firefighters, whilst attending operational incidents, are sometimes required to wear a breathing apparatus cylinder to help them breathe. It is very important that firefighters can calculate how much air is left in their cylinder. In order to work out how much air is left in a cylinder we need the following three pieces of information:

1. The time that the firefighter entered the fire.

2. How much air in minutes was in the cylinder when the firefighter entered the fire.

3. What the time is now.

Once you have these three pieces of information you will be able to work out how much air is left in the cylinder.

It is also advisable that you learn the 24-hour clock. We have provided you with a conversion chart to assist you during your preparation.

Conversion Chart

Here is a side-by-side comparison of the 24-hour clock and AM/PM:

0:00	12:00 Midnight	12:00	12:00 Noon
01:00	1:00 AM	13:00	1:00 PM
02:00	2:00 AM	14:00	2:00 PM
03:00	3:00 AM	15:00	3:00 PM
04:00	4:00 AM	16:00	4:00 PM
05:00	5:00 AM	17:00	5:00 PM
06:00	6:00 AM	18:00	6:00 PM
07:00	7:00 AM	19:00	7:00 PM
08:00	8:00 AM	20:00	8:00 PM
09:00	9:00 AM	21:00	9:00 PM
10:00	10:00 AM	22:00	10:00 PM
11:00	11:00 AM	23:00	11:00 PM

Before you sit the firefighter written tests, make sure you are competent in the use of the 24-hour clock and times that are in AM/PM.

Now take a look at the following sample working with numbers question:

Sample Question 1

The firefighter entered the fire at 19.09 and he had 47 minutes of air in his cylinder. The time is now 19.20. How much air does he have left?

A	B	C	D	E
32 minutes	33 minutes	34 minutes	35 minutes	36 minutes

The correct answer is E – 36 minutes.

Explanation – 11 minutes have now passed since the firefighter entered the building (19.20 – 19.09). To calculate how much air is left in the cylinder you need to subtract 11 minutes from the total amount of air that was in the cylinder when he entered the fire (47). Therefore, 47 -11 = 36 minutes.

Now try the sample exercise that follows. You have 5 minutes to answer the 10 questions. The correct answers are supplied at the end of the test.

Using Breathing Apparatus Sample Test

1. The firefighter entered the fire at 5.17am and he had 48 minutes of air in his cylinder. The time is now 5.30am. How much air does he have left?

A	B	C	D
35 minutes	53 minutes	30 minutes	34 minutes

2. The firefighter entered the fire at 17.30 and he had 42 minutes of air in his cylinder. The time is now 18.03. How much air does he have left?

A	B	C	D
39 minutes	9 minutes	7 minutes	33 minutes

3. The firefighter entered the fire at 8.01am and he had 39 minutes of air in his cylinder. The time is now 8.37am. How much air does he have left?

A	B	C	D
2 minutes	36 minutes	32 minutes	3 minutes

4. The time is now 23.05 and the firefighter had 45 minutes of air in her cylinder when she entered the fire at 23.04. How much air does she have left?

A	B	C	D
43 minutes	1 minute	2 minutes	44 minutes

5. The firefighter had 36 minutes of air in her cylinder when she entered the fire at 9.54pm. The time is now 10.15pm. How much air does she have left?

A	B	C	D
14 minutes	15 minutes	18 minutes	16 minutes

6. The time is now 5.26am and the firefighter had 39 minutes of air in his cylinder when he entered the fire at 5.05am. How much air does he have left?

A	B	C	D
18 minutes	1 minute	21 minutes	13 minutes

7. The firefighter had 38 minutes of air in her cylinder when she entered the fire at 16.02. The time is now 16.06. How much air does she have left?

A	B	C	D
4 minutes	34 minutes	36 minutes	14 minutes

8. The time is now 01.01 and the firefighter had 49 minutes of air in his cylinder when he entered the fire at 00.45. How much air does he have left?

A	B	C	D
4 minutes	44 minutes	33 minutes	48 minutes

9. The firefighter had 44 minutes of air in his cylinder when he entered the fire at 23.36. The time is now 00.03. How much air does he have left?

A	B	C	D
33 minutes	8 minutes	47 minutes	17 minutes

10. The time is now 2.07pm and the firefighter had 41 minutes of air in his cylinder when he entered the fire at 1.54pm. How much air does he have left?

A	B	C	D
7 minutes	13 minutes	28 minutes	9 minutes

Using Breathing Apparatus Test Answers

1. **A**

2. **B**

3. **D**

4. **D**

5. **B**

6. **A**

7. **B**

8. **C**

9. **D**

10. **C**

Tips for Passing this Test

You need to work on your numerical skills before you sit this test. After all, you are working with numbers. The tests in this guide are a great starting point. Any type of numerical reasoning test will be a good practice aid and there are plenty available at www.How2Become.com.

You will need to work quickly through each question and once again speed will only come with practice! Set aside 20 minutes each night in the 2 weeks before your test date and use this time to work on your numerical skills.

In order to assist you, please find 30 sample numerical test questions below this section that will improve your ability to pass the working with numbers test.

You are not permitted to use a calculator but you can use a rough sheet of paper in order to work out your calculations if you desire.

You have just 15 minutes to complete the test.

Practice Test – 30 Numerical Questions

1. **32 + ? = 66**

Answer:

2. **194 - ? = 33**

Answer:

3. **? + 112 = 218**

Answer:

4. **199 x ? = 796**

Answer:

5. **7 + 5 + 20 = 4 x ?**

Answer:

6. **(44 + 17) – 8 = ? + 4**

Answer:

7. **42 ÷ ? = 4 + 2**

Answer:

8. **3 x ? = 5 x 3**

Answer:

9. **100 ÷ 5 = 63 - ?**

Answer:

10. **45 x 8 = 720 ÷ ?**

Answer:

11. **Following the pattern shown in the number sequence below, what is the missing number represented by ?**

   4.5   9   18   ?   72   144

Answer:

12. **If you count from 1 to 100, how many 1s will you pass on the way?**

Answer:

13. **What is 10% of 250?**

Answer:

14. **What is 95% of 1000?**

Answer:

15. **111 + ? = 601**

Answer:

16. **48 - ? = 21**

Answer:

17. **? ÷ 222 = 5**

Answer:

18. **36 x ? = 324**

Answer:

19. **(12 + 3) x 3 = 5 x ?**

Answer:

20. **(16 + 32) − 8 = ? + 9**

Answer:

21. **29 x 6 = ?**

Answer:

22. **121 ÷ 11 = ?**

Answer:

23. A rectangle has an area of 36cm². The length of the longest side is 9cm. What is the length of the shortest side?

Answer:

24. A rectangle has an area of 48cm². The length of the longest side is 8cm. What is the perimeter of the rectangle?

Answer:

25. A square has an area of 144cm². What is the perimeter of the square?

Answer:

26. Is 99 divisible by 9?

Answer:

27. **What is 40% of 950?**

Answer: [   ]

28. **(60 – 18) x 2?**

Answer: [   ]

29. **(9 x 12) ÷ 2?**

Answer: [   ]

30. **(44 + 37) ÷ 9?**

Answer: [   ]

Now that you have completed this test, take the time to work through the answers carefully.

Practice Numerical Test Answers

1. 34
2. 161
3. 106
4. 4
5. 8
6. 49
7. 7
8. 5
9. 43
10. 2
11. 36
12. 21
13. 25
14. 950
15. 490
16. 27
17. 1110
18. 9
19. 9
20. 31
21. 174
22. 11
23. 4cm
24. 28cm
25. 48cm
26. Yes
27. 380
28. 84
29. 54
30. 9

As you will see from the 'working with numbers' test that relates to the use of breathing apparatus, it is essential that you are able to work quickly and accurately with the 24-hour clock and also the use of time. Once again, the following 30 questions are fantastic practice for the working with numbers test.

Work through the following questions as quickly as possible, and without the use of a calculator. You have just 10 minutes to complete the test. Use a blank sheet of paper to work out your answers if required. Write your answers down on the page, following the equals sign.

Practice Test – 30 More Numerical Questions

1. **27 minutes – 11 minutes =**

Answer: [   ]

2. **59 minutes – 12 minutes =**

Answer: [   ]

3. **48 minutes – 23 minutes =**

Answer: [   ]

4. **60 minutes – 31 minutes =**

Answer: [   ]

5. **47 minutes – 32 minutes =**

Answer: [   ]

6. **49 minutes – 11 minutes =**

Answer: [   ]

7. **14 minutes – 6 minutes =**

Answer: [   ]

8. **57 minutes – 12 minutes =**

Answer:

9. **54 minutes – 49 minutes =**

Answer:

10. **33 minutes – 9 minutes =**

Answer:

11. **43 minutes – 33 minutes =**

Answer:

12. **60 minutes – 42 minutes =**

Answer:

13. **18 minutes – 7 minutes =**

Answer:

14. **13 minutes – 8 minutes =**

Answer:

15. **26 minutes – 7 minutes =**

Answer:

16. **11 minutes – 2 minutes =**

Answer:

17. **17 minutes – 5 minutes =**

Answer:

18. **7 minutes – 2 minutes =**

Answer:

19. **1 hour 43 minutes – 1 hour 12 minutes =**

Answer:

20. **1 hour 16 minutes – 55 minutes =**

Answer:

21. **1 hour 59 minutes – 1 hour 33 minutes =**

Answer:

22. **2 hours 3 minutes – 1 hour 15 minutes =**

Answer: [ ]

23. **2 hours 27 minutes – 1 hour 26 minutes =**

Answer: [ ]

24. **2 hours 41 minutes – 1 hour 14 minutes =**

Answer: [ ]

25. **2 hours 14 minutes – 1 hour 41 minutes =**

Answer: [ ]

26. **4 hours 9 minutes – 2 hour 59 minutes =**

Answer: [ ]

27. **3 hours 34 minutes – 2 hour 43 minutes =**

Answer: [ ]

28. **2 hours 44 minutes – 45 minutes =**

Answer: [ ]

29. **5 hours 1 minute – 1 hour 5 minutes =**

Answer:

30. **3 hours 13 minutes – 2 hours 58 minutes =**

Answer:

Now that you have completed the test, take your time to work through the answers carefully.

Practice Numerical Test Answers

1. 16 minutes

2. 47 minutes

3. 25 minutes

4. 29 minutes

5. 15 minutes

6. 38 minutes

7. 8 minutes

8. 45 minutes

9. 5 minutes

10. 24 minutes

11. 10 minutes

12. 18 minutes

13. 11 minutes

14. 5 minutes

15. 19 minutes

16. 9 minutes

17. 12 minutes

18. 5 minutes

19. 31 minutes

20. 21 minutes

21. 26 minutes

22. 48 minutes

23. 1 hour 1 minute (61 minutes)

24. 1 hour 27 minutes (87 minutes)

25. 33 minutes

26. 1 hour 10 minutes (70 minutes)

27. 51 minutes

28. 1 hour 59 minutes (119 minutes)

29. 3 hours 56 minutes (236 minutes)

30. 15 minutes

Further Sample Questions – Working with Numbers Test

Now that you have had chance to practise some breathing apparatus test questions, and you have taken the time to work through the additional numerical test questions, take a look at the following sample questions that relate to your ability to interpret graphs and charts.

There is a total of 10 questions in this test, and you have 15 minutes in which to complete it.

(Please note: the statistics shown are fictional, created solely for these practice questions.)

1. The following graph details information about how many people died from house fires during a 12-month period in Town A.

How many people died in homes without smoke alarms during the 12-month period?

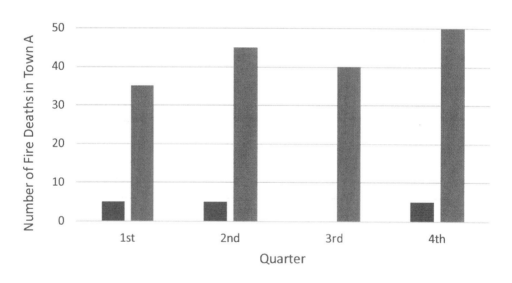

Homes with Smoke Alarms

Homes without Smoke Alarms

Answer:

2. The following graph details information about how many people died from house fires during a 12-month period in Town B.

How many people in total died in house fires during the 12-month period?

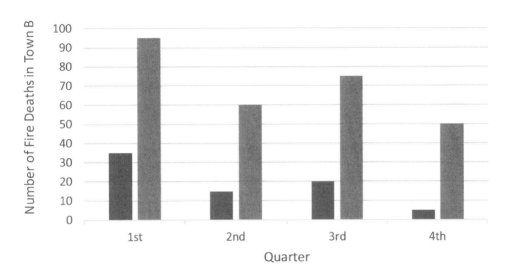

Answer:

3. The following graph details information about how many people died from house fires during a 12-month period in Town C.

On average, how many people died in homes with a smoke alarm each month during the 12-month period?

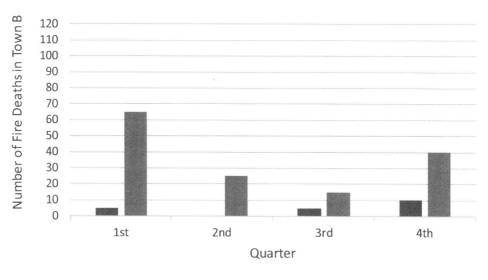

Answer: [   ]

4. You have been asked by your Watch Manager at the Fire Station to clean the following rooms: the basement, the kitchen and the training suite. A floor plan of the total area you are required to clean is detailed below (not to scale).

Basement: 60 square metres

Training Suite: 68 square metres

Kitchen: 53 square metres

What is the total floor area you are required to clean?

Answer:

5. You have been asked by your Watch Manager at the Fire Station to clean the following rooms: the basement, the kitchen and the training suite. A floor plan of the total area you are required to clean is detailed below (not to scale).

Kitchen: 53 square metres

Basement: 60 square metres

Training Suite: 68 square metres

If you were to clean 1 square metre every 30 seconds, how long would it take you to clean the training suite?

Answer:

6. You have been asked by your Watch Manager at the Fire Station to clean the appliance bay floor. A floor plan of the total area you are required to clean is detailed below (not to scale).

Appliance Bay: 280 square metres

If one bucket of cleaning fluid will clean 20 square metres of floor, how many buckets will you need to clean half of the appliance bay floor area?

Answer:

7. You have been asked by your Watch Manager at the Fire Station to clean the appliance bay floor and the kitchen floor. A floor plan of the total area you are required to clean is detailed below (not to scale).

Kitchen: 180 square metres	Appliance Bay: 320 square metres

If one bucket of cleaning fluid will clean 20 square metres of floor, how many buckets will you need to clean a quarter of the appliance bay floor and all of the kitchen floor area?

Answer:

8. Firefighters attend many different types of fire including rubbish fires, car fires and grass fires. The graph below provides details of these types of fires within the area covered by one particular station over a four-week period. Use the graph to answer the question below.

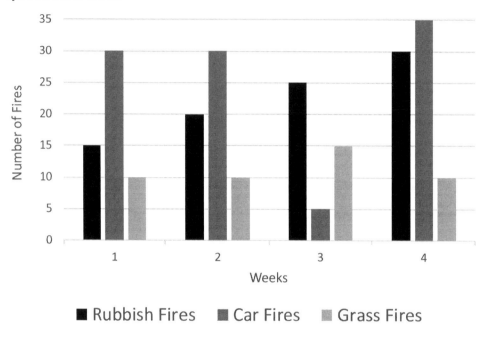

What was the combined number of rubbish fires and car fires in weeks 3 and 4?

Answer:

9. Firefighters attend many different types of fire including rubbish fires, car fires and grass fires. The graph below provides details of these types of fires within the area covered by one particular station over a four-week period. Use the graph to answer the question below.

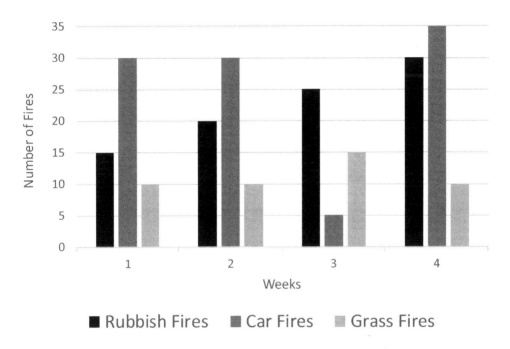

Firefighters often carry out intensive Fire Safety campaigns in order to reduce the number of calls they attend. If firefighters had been carrying out this type of campaign during the four-week period above, which category of fires and in which week did the campaign have the most positive effect?

Answer:

10. Firefighters attend many different types of fire including rubbish fires, car fires and grass fires. The graph below provides details of these types of fires within the area covered by one particular station over a four-week period. Use the graph to answer the question below.

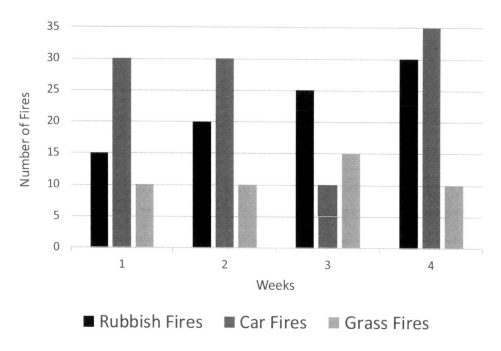

■ Rubbish Fires   ■ Car Fires   ▨ Grass Fires

What was the average number of fires attended by the station each week?

Answer:

Further Sample Questions – Working with Numbers Answers

1. 170

2. 355

3. 20

4. 181 square metres

5. 34 minutes

6. 7 buckets

7. 13 buckets

8. 95 fires

9. Car fires; week 3

10. 60 fires

Sample Numerical Tests

As you have probably gathered, being able to work with basic numerical calculations is vital to your success during the firefighter selection process. A great way to prepare for the working with numbers test is to carry out plenty of numerical reasoning tests. If you would like more sample test questions then you need to obtain a copy of a numerical reasoning test book from www.How2Become.com. Remember, practice makes perfect.

On the following pages please find even more useful numerical questions to help you prepare for your tests.

Allow yourself 10 minutes to complete the 30 questions and do not use a calculator. You are permitted to use a blank sheet of paper to carry out your calculations if required.

More Practice Numerical Tests

1. 9 minutes multiplied by 35 = ?

(Provide your answer in hours and minutes)

Answer:

2. 22 minutes multiplied by 6 = ?

(Provide your answer in hours and minutes)

Answer:

3. (9 x 15) – 12 = ?

Answer:

4. 112 ÷ ? = 2 x 28

Answer:

5. (6 + 6) x 15 = 15 x ?

Answer:

6. (39 - 34) – 4 = ? + 1

Answer:

7. 14 minutes multiplied by 17 = ?

(Provide your answer in hours and minutes)

Answer: [ ]

8. 1440 minutes divided by 5 = ?

(Provide your answer in hours and minutes)

Answer: [ ]

9. 45% of 200 = ?

Answer: [ ]

10. 98% of 300 = ?

Answer: [ ]

11. 5% of 30 = ?

Answer: [ ]

12. 4 x 4.5 = ?

Answer: [ ]

13. 90 x 20% = ?

Answer: [ ]

14. 120 x 15% = ?

Answer: [ ]

15. You are attending a fire in a house and the nearest fire hydrant is 170 metres away. The hose that you are carrying on the fire engine comes in 23 metre lengths. How many lengths will you need to reach the fire hydrant?

Answer: [ ]

16. You are attending a fire in a block of flats and the nearest fire hydrant is 150 metres away. The hose that you are carrying on the fire engine comes in 23 metre lengths. How many lengths will you need to reach the fire hydrant?

Answer: [ ]

17. Firefighters are required to pitch their ladders a third of the working height away from a building? If the working height is 12 metres, how far away from the building will you pitch the ladder?

Answer: [ ]

18. Firefighters are sometimes required to lift water from ponds, canals and rivers. In order to gain a sufficient lift, the suction hose used must be submerged at least 3 times it's diameter below the surface of the water.

    If the suction hose that you are using is 12.5 cm in diameter, to what level (minimum) must it be submerged?

Answer:

19. If a firefighter trains for 25 minutes per day, for 5 days per week, how many hours and minutes will he have trained for over a 5 week period?

Answer:

20. If a firefighter trains for 23 minutes per day, for 6 days per week, how many hours and minutes will he have trained for over a 7 week period?

Answer:

21. A Fire and Rescue Service purchases 8 fire engines at a cost of £289,000 each. In total, how much have they spent on fire engines?

Answer:

22. A Fire and Rescue Service purchases 6 fire engines at a cost of £276,000 each. In addition to this, they purchase a servicing plan for each engine at a cost of £13,850 each. In total, how much have they spent on fire engines and servicing plans?

Answer:

23.   If a firefighter earns a consistent annual salary of £26,432, how much will she earn in 6 years?

Answer: [   ]

24. There are 50 fire stations in the county of Marshshire. If the total number of firefighters serving on fire stations across the entire county is 2000, what is the average number of firefighters serving at each station?

Answer: [   ]

25. Larningshire Fire and Rescue Service attends 47,000 fires during 2007/08. If, during the following year it attends 20% less fires, how many fires will it attend?

Answer: [   ]

26. Bottomsgate Fire and Rescue Service attends 62,000 fires during 2007/08. If, during the following year it attends 25% less fires, how many fires will it attend?

Answer: [   ]

27. Firefighters are required to pitch their ladders a third of the working height away from a building? If the working height is 21 metres, how far away from the building will you pitch the ladder?

Answer: [   ]

28. Murkdale Fire and Rescue Service attended 33,000 fires during 2009/10. If, during the previous year it attended 30% more fires, how many fires did it attend?

Answer:

29. Duttingford Fire and Rescue Service attended 29,046 fires during 2009/10, whilst neighbouring county Morkdale attended 33,117. How many more fires did Morkdale attend compared with Duttingford?

Answer:

30. Greyshire Fire and Rescue Service attended 30,500 fires during 2008/09. During the following year, it attended 36,600 fires. What is the increase as a percentage?

Answer:

More Practice Numerical Tests - Answers

1. 5 hours and fifteen minutes

2. 2 hours and twelve minutes

3. 123

4. 2

5. 12

6. 0

7. 3 hours and 58 minutes

8. 4 hours and 48 minutes

9. 90

10. 294

11. 1.5

12. 18

13. 18

14. 18

15. 8 lengths

16. 7 lengths

17. 4 metres

18. 37.5 cm

19. 10 hours and 25 minutes

20. 16 hours and 6 minutes

21. £2,312,000

22. £1,739,100

23. £158,592

24. 40

25. 37,600 fires

26. 46,500 fires

27. 7 metres

28. 42,900 fires

29. 4071 fires

30. 20%

Chapter 3
Understanding Information

The Understanding Information test is designed to assess your ability to learn and retain information. Firefighters need to be capable of learning lots of job specific information. They also need to be able to retain that information so that they can use it during training and whilst attending operational incidents.

There are plenty of policies and procedures to learn and you will also need to be fully conversant with the operating manuals for your equipment and your Personal Protective Equipment (PPE). If you can successfully pass this test then there is a good chance that you will be able to apply the same skills to the role of a firefighter. During this test you will be presented with a written passage and it is your job to read the text carefully before answering a series of questions based on the information provided.

You may also find that the information provided is presented by video or in verbal format. If this is the case then you may be permitted to take notes during the presentation. After reading the passage, your options are true, false or Cannot say based on the information provided. Remember to answer the questions based solely on the information provided and do not make the mistake of assuming.

On the following pages, please find a number of short passages followed by a series of questions for you to answer. Remember to base your responses solely on the information provided. During questions 25 onwards, instead of answering 'true', 'false', or 'cannot say', you will be required to select the correct answer from a selection of 4 options. This is how the questions will be during the actual test.

Please circle the correct answer. You have 60 minutes to complete all 50 questions.

Tips for the Understanding Information Test

1. **Read everything carefully.**

Now this is an obvious one, but don't get caught out by any wording either in the prompt passage or the questions themselves. For example, watch out for questions that may be worded in potentially deceiving ways.

Of course, the answer to a question beginning 'The role of the firefighter contains…' will be very different to a question beginning 'The role of the firefighter does not contain…'

In short, make sure you're saying what you want to say with your responses!

2. **Be honest.**

As you read through the questions, you will quickly realise what recruiters want to see from your answers. For example, you will have to say you enjoy working hard and rising to challenges.

So, while you are liable to fail if you do not respond in this manner, you should always be as honest as you can. If you are not, you risk being found out at a later stage of the process, or worse – once you have been recruited.

3. **Remember the PQAs.**

This is probably the most important tip of them all – when responding, you must have the PQAs in mind at all times. They are the metrics by which you assessed at every stage of the process, so get acquainted with the ones set out by your chosen Fire and Rescue Service.

In the sample responses to an Understanding Information Test provided later, this will be stressed again, with accompanying responses you can use to get an idea of how to do this.

Now, read on to undertake a sample Understanding Information Test.

Understanding Information Exercise

Disclaimer - Although some of the information within the passages relates to fire safety and firefighter procedures, it should not relied upon as an accurate source of information to prevent fires or otherwise.

Read the following passage before answering the questions that follow based on the information provided.

The role of a firefighter can be extremely demanding. Not only will you be called upon to attend building fires, rubbish fires, car fires and grass fires, but you will also be required to deal with chemical spills. During every incident the firefighter must remain calm and focused on the task in hand.

There is no room for complacency and each firefighter must ensure that they keep up-to-date with training and operational procedures. Firefighters are also required to wear personal protective equipment (PPE) whilst attending operational incidents. Their PPE must be maintained to a high standard so that it is available for operational readiness at all times.

In addition to attending operational incidents, the modern-day firefighter will work closely with the local community. part of this role includes educating the public against the dangers of fire in the home, advising local businesses and fitting smoke alarms in homes that are most at risk from fire. the role of a firefighter is one that requires dedication, commitment, adaptability and a high degree of professionalism.

1. Firefighters are required to maintain their fitness levels for operational readiness.

        A. True   **B. False**   **C. Cannot say**

2. Part of the role of a firefighter includes educating the public against the dangers of fire in the home.

        A. True   **B. False**   **C. Cannot say**

3. There is room for complacency as a firefighter.

        A. True   **B. False**   **C. Cannot say**

4. In addition to attending operational incidents, the modern-day firefighter will work closely with the local authority.

   A. True   **B. False**   **C. Cannot say**

5. The role of a firefighter can be extremely dangerous.

   A. True   **B. False**   **C. Cannot say**

6. Firefighters are required to wear PPE whilst attending operational incidents.

   A. True   **B. False**   **C. Cannot say**

7. In addition to attending building fires, rubbish fires, car fires and grass fires, firefighters will also have to attend road traffic collisions.

   A. True   **B. False**   **C. Cannot say**

8. Part of the firefighter's role includes educating the public against the dangers of fire in the home, advising local businesses and fitting smoke alarms in homes that are least at risk from fire.

   A. True   **B. False**   **C. Cannot say**

Read the following passage before answering the questions below based on the information provided.

Retained firefighters are a crucial part of the Fire & rescue service. In order to be eligible to become a retained firefighter, applicants must normally reside or work within five minutes of the fire station. This ensures that they are available to attend incidents as and when required.

Retained fire stations are usually based in rural areas where a wholetime fire station would not be cost effective. Retained firefighters wear a pager whilst on duty, which allows them to be alerted to a fire or incident from the central Fire Service Control Centre. Once the pager is activated, the retained firefighter will then proceed to the fire station where he or she will mount the fire engine before proceeding to the incident. The role of a retained firefighter requires a high degree of flexibility, dedication and commitment.

Often, retained firefighters are on duty for many hours at a time, providing essential cover to their local community. Finally, it is vital that the retained firefighter has a flexible and understanding employer, as they are often required to attend emergency incidents during working hours.

9. In order to be eligible to become a retained firefighter, applicants must be over 18.

A. True   B. False   C. Cannot say

10. Retained firefighters are required to wear Personal Protective Equipment, just like their wholetime firefighter colleagues.

A. True   B. False   C. Cannot say

11. Once the pager is activated, the retained firefighter will then proceed directly to the incident.

A. True   B. False   C. Cannot say

12. It is vital that the retained firefighter has a flexible and understanding employer, as they are often required to attend training sessions during working hours.

A. True   B. False   C. Cannot say

13. The role of a retained firefighter requires a high degree of commitment.

A. True   B. False   C. Cannot say

14. In order to be eligible to become a retained firefighter, applicants must normally reside or work within five hours of the fire station.

           A. True   **B. False**   **C. Cannot say**

15. Retained firefighters wear a pager.

           A. True   **B. False**   **C. Cannot say**

16. Retained firefighters are often required to attend incidents during the evening.

           A. True   **B. False**   **C. Cannot say**

Read the following passage before answering the questions below based on the information provided.

Upon successful completion of the firefighter recruitment and application process, successful candidates will be provided with a course date and a location for which their initial training will take place. The first phase of training is entitled phase I and lasts for 15 weeks in total.

During phase I training, firefighters will learn the basic foundations of the role, including the use of firefighting hose, the use of ladders and the use of pumps. 35% of phase I training is classroom based, with the remainder taking place on the drill ground or training areas. once the firefighter has successfully completed phase I training, they will then commence the training of wearing breathing apparatus.

This is a 4-week course which provides the basic fundamental principles for operating and wearing breathing apparatus in a safe and effective manner. Firefighters will learn the operational procedures for wearing Breathing apparatus before being put through their paces in the fire house.

Once Breathing apparatus training is complete, firefighters will then undertake modules that are centred on road traffic collisions, risk assessment and First aid. throughout the duration of their training, firefighters will learn the important subject of Community safety. They will also get the opportunity to attend local schools where they have the chance to give presentations to the school children on the importance of fire safety, how to dial 999 and why they must not make hoax calls.

In addition to technical lectures and practical sessions, firefighters will be assessed by way of written and practical assessments throughout the duration of their training. Firefighters must pass each assessment in order to progress through the course.

17. 75% of Phase 1 training takes place on the drill ground or training areas.

A. True   B. False   C. Cannot say

18. Firefighters will be assessed by way of written and practical assessments during phase 1 of their training only.

A. True   B. False   C. Cannot say

19. First aid training immediately follows Phase 1 training.

      A. True   **B. False**   **C. Cannot say**

20. During their training, firefighters will give presentations to school children on how to make hoax calls.

      A. True   **B. False**   **C. Cannot say**

21. Risk assessment training follows Breathing Apparatus training.

      A. True   **B. False**   **C. Cannot say**

22. During Breathing Apparatus training, firefighters are required to wear Personal Protective Equipment (PPE).

      A. True   **B. False**   **C. Cannot say**

23. 65% of Phase 1 training takes place on the drill ground or training areas.

      A. True   **B. False**   **C. Cannot say**

24. If a firefighter fails an assessment, they will be required to re-sit it.

      A. True   **B. False**   **C. Cannot say**

Read the following passage before answering the questions below based on the information provided.

A risk assessment is an important step in protecting firefighters from risk of harm, injury or death. it also allows the Fire and rescue service to comply with the law. the main purpose of a risk assessment is to allow employees to identify the hazards and risks that have the potential to cause harm.

By being aware of the risks and hazards, a firefighter can take appropriate action to eliminate, control or reduce them. as an example, whilst walking around the fire station, a firefighter notices that there has been an oil spillage on the floor. to reduce the risk, or to eliminate it totally, the firefighter may decide to clean the oil spillage and ensure that the surface is dry. this will reduce the risk of anyone slipping on the spill and subsequently injuring themselves.

If the spillage was constant, i.e. from a leaking pipe, the firefighter may decide to place appropriate warning signs in the vicinity of the spill in order to pre-warn people of the hazard. although this course of action would not eliminate the risk, it would reduce it. the law does not expect employees and employers to eliminate all risk, however, you are required to protect people as far as is 'reasonably practicable'.

25. From reading the passage, which statement is true?

 A) The law expects employees and employers to eliminate all risk.

 B) The law does not expect employees and employers to eliminate risk.

 C) Employees and employers are not required by law to eliminate all risk.

 D) The law does not expect employees and employers to eliminate risk.

26. A risk assessment:

 A) Allows the Fire and Rescue Service to employ people.

 B) Encourages people to be safe at work.

 C) Allows the Fire and Rescue Service to comply with the law.

 D) Reduces the risk of broken bones.

27. The main purpose of a risk assessment is to:

A) Make employers and employees comply with the law.

B) Allow employees to identify the hazards and risks that have the potential to cause harm.

C) Clean up spillages.

D) To protect people by being 'reasonably practicable'.

28. To eliminate the risk of an oil spillage in the fire station floor, the firefighter may decide to:

A) Place warning signs in the vicinity of the spill.

B) Stop the leak.

C) Clean up the spillage.

D) Inform the line manager.

Read the following passage before answering the questions below based on the information provided.

The process for calling 999 is a simple one, however, when it comes to it, many people are unsure. The first step is to find the nearest telephone. it does not matter if you have no minutes left on your phone, or even if there is no reception, the call can still be made.

All you need to do is lift the receiver and dial 999. once the call is made, the first person that you will speak to is the operator. Give the operator your phone number, or the number you are dialling from, and ask for the Fire service.

After a short dialling tone, you will be put through to the nearest Fire Control Centre. From here, a qualified call handler will deal with your call. throughout the call it is important that you remain calm, speak clearly and provide as much information as possible about the incident. the call operator will ask you questions such as:

• What incident are you reporting?

• Where is the incident?

• What telephone number are you calling from?

More often than not, the operator will ask you to provide relevant information such as prominent landmarks, main roads, postcodes, or any other information that you may feel will assist the Fire and Rescue Service to locate the incident.

29. The first thing you should do is:

A) Provide as much information as possible about the incident.

B) Find the nearest telephone.

C) Remain calm.

D) Dial 999.

30. The first person that you will communicate with is:

A) The fire station closest to the incident.

B) A Fire and Rescue Service call handler.

C) The operator.

D) An automated answer message.

31. If you have no credit on your phone:

A) You will not be able to dial 999.

B) You can make a 999 call but you only have 2 minutes to speak to the operator.

C) You cannot dial 999.

D) You can still dial 999 and make the call.

32. Which of the following is not true?

A) Throughout the call it is important that you remain calm, speak clearly and provide as much information as possible about the incident.

B) The process for calling 999 is a simple one.

C) If you have no credit on your phone, or if there is no reception, the call cannot be made.

D) Once the call is made, the first person that you will speak to is the operator.

Read the following passage before answering the questions below based on the information provided.

Equality and diversity are important aspects of the Fire service. equality is all about respect and not treating an individual or group of people unfairly or with discrimination. this applies to people both within the service itself and also across the local communities which the Fire and rescue service serves.

The Fire and rescue service will give its employees an equality of opportunity. This essentially means that everybody will be given the opportunity to fulfil their potential, regardless of their age, sex, background, religion, disability, sexual orientation or otherwise. Equality is based on the idea of fairness while recognising everyone is different. Diversity is about the ways in which people, both within the service and within the local community, differ.

It is also about recognising that these differences are a natural and positive part of society. Diversity means people should be treated as individuals and it is important that those people feel respected and valued. there are, of course, many myths about equality and diversity. some people believe that it is about giving certain groups an unfair advantage, or simply to be seen as being 'politically correct'. in fact, these myths couldn't be further from the truth.

It is about treating people fairly and having respect for individuals and groups. true equality can only come about as a result of positive attitudes to diversity and the needs of individuals, rather than from treating everyone the same.

The Fire and rescue service strive to treat everyone fairly, equally and with utmost respect. Because the Fire and rescue service plays an important part in the local community, it is essential that equality and diversity are both at the forefront of its plans, policies and beliefs. the Fire and rescue service do not discriminate against anyone because of their colour, race, back- ground, nationality, ethnic origin, religious beliefs, disability, age, sex, gender identity, marital status or sexual orientation.

33. Equality and diversity is:

A) About treating people fairly and having respect for individuals and groups.

B) Differences.

C) About being politically correct.

D) About treating people as they ask to be treated.

34. Which of the following statements is true?

A) Employees will give their employer an equality of opportunity.

B) The Fire and Rescue Service will occasionally discriminate against people.

C) Positive attitudes to diversity and the needs of individuals, rather than from treating everyone the same will lead to true equality.

D) The Fire and Rescue Service strive to treat everyone fairly, equally and with utmost respect by paying them equal wages.

35. Myths about equality and diversity include:

A) Treating people fairly and having respect for individuals and groups.

B) Not giving certain groups an unfair advantage.

C) To be seen as being 'politically correct'.

D) Discrimination, bullying and harassment.

Read the following passage before answering the questions below based on the information provided.

Firefighters are sometimes confronted with extremely dangerous situations involving flashover and/or backdraught. let's assume that a fire is still burning within a room or compartment and there is nowhere for the combustible gases to escape.

When the door is opened, the immediate influx of fresh air will mix with the combustible gases and create an explosive mixture. if the combustible gases that are present within the compartment are hot enough, they will ignite and the resultant flame will spread back into the compartment/room along with the fresh air.

Alternatively, if the gases are not hot enough to cause auto-ignition, they will only ignite once sufficient oxygen has reached the combustible gases that surround the fire. this dangerous situation will inevitably result in a fast and rapid growth of fire. The firefighter must be well trained and fully prepared for such eventualities. spotting the signs of flashover and backdraught before they occur will enable the firefighter to take sufficient action(s) to reduce the risk within the compartment or room.

36. An explosive mixture is created when:

A) The fire is still burning within the compartment or room.

B) The door is opened in a room or compartment which involves a fire and there is nowhere for the combustible gases to escape.

C) A firefighter fails to spot the warning signs.

D) Firefighters are confronted with extremely dangerous situations involving flashover and/or backdraught.

37. From reading the passage it is true that:

A) If a firefighter fails to spot the signs of flashover and backdraught they will die.

B) Fresh air entering a room or compartment through an open door will mix with the combustible gases to create an explosive mixture.

C) Gases that are not hot enough to cause auto-ignition will only ignite once limited oxygen has reached the combustible gases that surround the fire.

D) Firefighters must wear Personal Protective Equipment if they are to be safe whilst fighting the fire.

Read the following passage before answering the questions below based on the information provided.

The predetermined attendance (PDA) for a road traffic collision (RTC), where one or more casualties are trapped inside the vehicle is as follows – two fire engines, with at least one of them carrying suitable hydraulic rescue equipment, with a minimum of 4 firefighters on board per engine. this will ensure that at least 8 firefighters will be at the scene to carry out the rescue(s).

The fire engine that carries the hydraulic rescue equipment is usually called a water tender ladder, or rescue water tender ladder in some counties. Fire engines that do not carry any hydraulic rescue equipment are usually called water tenders. in addition to the attendance of two fire engines, an officer will be mobilised.

It is the officer's responsibility to oversee and direct operations within accordance of the Fire service policies and operational procedures. If the incident involves larger vehicles such as lorries or buses, then the PDA will be enhanced. In addition to the two fire engines, again one of the two pumps being a water tender ladder, a specialist rescue unit will be deployed.

This special Unit will carry far more sophisticated lifting and cutting equipment, and even in some cases an infra-red search camera that can be used to detect the location of severely trapped casualties. This type of vehicle will be crewed by a specially trained team of firefighters.

Once again, an officer of suitable experience and rank will be deployed to the scene to oversee operations.

38. The Predetermined Attendance (PDA) for a road traffic collision (RTC), where one or more casualties are trapped inside the vehicle, involves:

A) A total of 8 personnel.

B) Two fire engines, one officer and one specialist unit.

C) A total of 9 personnel.

D) A special unit carrying sophisticated lifting and cutting equipment. In some cases an infra-red search camera will be carried so that it can be used to detect the location of severely trapped casualties.

39. From reading the passage it is true that:

A) Hydraulic rescue equipment is usually carried on a Water Tender.

B) An officer will be deployed to the Control Centre to oversee operations.

C) Specially trained firefighters crew the Special Unit.

D) Fire engines that do not carry any hydraulic rescue equipment are usually called Water Tenders Ladders.

40. The passage is about:

A) The attendance of fire engines and personnel to different Road Traffic Collisions (RTC).

B) The equipment carried on fire engines that attend Road Traffic Collisions (RTC).

C) The differences in the Predetermined Attendances (PDA) for 'severe' and 'not so severe' Road Traffic Collisions (RTC).

D) The equipment carried on Special Units.

Read the following passage before answering the questions below based on the information provided.

Firefighting in high–rise buildings is often a complex and difficult task. Fires in these types of buildings are often unpredictable and hard to locate. once the initial attendance arrives at the scene, the incident Commander should make an immediate assessment of the risks (Dynamic risk assessment).

As soon as he has gathered all of the relevant facts pertaining to the incident, such as location of the fire, persons involved or missing, wind direction, location of water supplies, severity of the fire etc, he will then proceed directly to the floor which is located below the fire. with him there will be a breathing apparatus team and one additional firefighter who will operate the Entry Control Board (ECB).

Following a further Dynamic risk assessment, the incident Commander must then set up a bridgehead which will be used for firefighter operations and tactics. During incidents of this nature, firefighting operations should never start on the floor of the fire. they should always be started on a suitable floor below the fire, in fresh air.

Once the bridgehead is established, a firefighter (who will have the use of a radio) should be nominated to take control of the lifts within the high–rise block. the lifts must not be used by the general public during a fire. in order for the nominated firefighter to take control of the lift, he/she must operate the ' firefighter's switch'.

This will then give the firefighter total control of the lift from the ground floor. the nominated firefighter, in liaison with the incident Commander, will ensure the required personnel and equipment are deployed to the correct scene of operations using the lift.

Whilst all of the above is taking place, the driver of the first fire engine will run out lengths of hose from the fire engine to the rising main. the hose lines to the rising main will only be charged on the instructions of the incident Commander. it is essential that good communications are maintained between the incident Commander and his crew.

41. The article is about:

  A) Carrying out a Dynamic Risk Assessment.

  B) Firefighting procedures in high rise buildings.

C) Communications from the bridgehead.

D) The operation of lifts during fires.

42. The hose lines from the fire engine to the rising main:

A) Will be charged as soon as they are connected.

B) Will be charged by the driver of the first fire engine when he is ready.

C) Will be charged when the Incident Commander gives his instruction to charge them.

D) As soon as the bridgehead has been established.

43. During incidents involving fires in high rise buildings, firefighting operations should:

A) Be set up on the floor immediately above the location of the fire.

B) Commence immediately after the lifts have been secured by the firefighter's switch.

C) Be started in fresh air on a suitable floor below the fire.

D) Be set up on the floor of the fire.

44. Which of the following is not true?

A) The first task, upon arrival at the incident, is for the Incident Commander to carry out a Dynamic Risk Assessment (DRA).

B) The bridgehead is always set up below the floor of the fire.

C) The driver of the first fire engine will run out lengths of hose from the hydrant to the rising main. The rising main will only then be charged once the Incident Commander gives instruction to.

D) The nominated firefighter can take control of the lifts by operating the 'firefighter's switch'.

Read the following passage before answering the questions below based on the information provided.

The 'responsible person' is a person who has a level of control over the fire precaution measures for the building or business premise. this might be the owner of the building, the managing agent or another designated person.

The responsible person has a legal duty to ensure that employees, visitors or contractors working in the premise, or anyone else who is on the premise at any given time, can safely escape in the event of a fire. The responsible person must make sure they take into account vulnerable people such as the disabled, the young, the elderly or anyone who requires special attention/care. The responsible person, in carrying out their duties, must carry out a fire risk assessment.

The purpose of the fire risk assessment is to identify the risks, and the hazards associated with those risks, before taking appropriate action to reduce, minimise or eradicate the risks. the findings of the risk assessment must then be made available to everyone on the premise.

The responsible person must take all reasonable measures to put in place fire precautions to deal with any risks that remain following the fire risk assessment. the responsible person has the right to nominate a competent person to carry out the fire risk assessment but they are still responsible in law, regardless of who actually carries out the assessment.

45. The article is about:

A) The duties of the responsible person.

B) The risk assessment process.

C) The legal duties of employees in business premises.

D) Vulnerable people in business premises.

46. Which of the following is not true?

A) Following the risk assessment, the responsible person must not take all reasonable measures to put in place fire precautions to deal with any risks that remain.

B) The responsible person must carry out a risk assessment.

C) The responsible person can nominate a competent person to carry out the fire risk assessment.

D) The purpose of the fire risk assessment is to identify the risks, and the hazards associated with those risks.

47. It is true that:

A) The risk assessment must be carried out by the responsible person.

B) The findings of the risk assessment must then be made available to everyone on the premise.

C) The responsible person must take all reasonable measures to install fire extinguishers.

D) The responsible person is the person who owns the building.

Read the following passage before answering the questions below based on the information provided.

Before you can start your training as a firefighter you will need to pass a medical. The medical is usually carried out by the Fire and rescue service doctor on a Fire service establishment and will take approximately 60 minutes to complete.

Before the medical can commence, the doctor will need to have access to your medical records. this will allow him/her to assess your medical history to ascertain whether there are any problems that could prevent you from fulfilling a long and healthy career within the Fire service.

As soon as you arrive at the medical you will be asked to complete a comprehensive questionnaire which will provide details about your health, lifestyle and medical history. You may also be required to provide a urine sample. in no particular order, you will be required to undergo a series of tests as follows:

Hearing Test – this is where you will be asked to sit in a sound proofed booth whilst wearing headphones. You will hear a series of short tones in each ear of differing levels and frequencies. it is your task to identify when you hear a tone, and also which ear you can hear the tone in.

Chester Step Test – you will be required to step up and down on a box which is usually 12 inches in height. whilst you are performing the step test your heart rate will be monitored.

Lung Function Test – this test requires you to blow long and hard into a plastic tube until you have fully expended all air within your lungs. a reading is then taken to assess the functionality of your lungs and their capacity.

Strength Test – you will be required to squat on a machine which will assess your back and leg strength.

Finally, the doctor will carry out a series of further small tests to assess your overall medical and fitness condition. the medical takes approximately one hour to complete.

48. Which of the following is true?

A) There are four tests in total during the medical.

B) A plastic tube is used during the Chester Step Test.

C) The medical cannot commence until the doctor has access to the medical records.

D) Most people pass the medical.

49. The medical history will:

A) Identify to the doctor whether there are any problems that could prevent you from fulfilling a long and healthy career within the Fire Service.

B) Take a while to come back from the applicant's real doctor.

C) Stay with the Fire Service after the medical is complete.

D) Provide the results of the applicant's previous Chester Step test, strength test, hearing test and lung function test.

50. Which of the following is not true?

A) The strength test assesses back and leg strength.

B) The medical takes approximately 60 minutes to complete.

C) During the Chester Step test the heart rate is monitored.

D) During the medical, the tests are always carried out in the following order:

    1. Hearing Test

    2. Chester Step Test

    3. Lung Function Test

    4. Strength Test

Understanding Information Exercise - Answers

1. Cannot say	26. C
2. True	27. B
3. False	28. C
4. Cannot say	29. B
5. Cannot say	30. C
6. True	31. D
7. Cannot say	32. C
8. False	33. A
9. Cannot say	34. C
10. Cannot say	35. C
11. False	36. B
12. Cannot say	37. B
13. True	38. C
14. False	39. C
15. True	40. A
16. Cannot say	41. B
17. False	42. C
18. False	43. C
19. False	44. C
20. False	45. A
21. True	46. A
22. Cannot say	47. B
23. True	48. C
24. Cannot say	49. A
25. C	50. D

Chapter 4
Situational Awareness and Problem Solving

This test assesses an applicant's ability to ensure the safety of themselves and others and also their ability to use information in order to solve problems.

The test requires you to read descriptions of situations or scenarios that you are likely to face when working as a firefighter. You will then be presented with four alternative answers and you must choose the answer that most closely describes what you would do in that situation. It is important to understand that firefighters must be capable of working both safely and unsupervised. Answer the questions carefully and think about the scenario before you respond.

The real test has 30 questions and you will have 35 minutes to complete them. It is up to you to read each question very carefully before selecting your answer. Before you try the sample test, take a look at the following example test question.

Example Test Question – Situational Awareness and Problem Solving

Whilst on duty, you overhear a conversation between two firefighters. One of them is making inappropriate comments about the other firefighter's gender. What would you do?

  A. Ignore the comments and carry on with my work. Banter is part and parcel of Fire Service life.

  B. Join in with the comments. It's only a bit of fun and if the other person cannot take it, then they shouldn't be in the job.

  C. Immediately challenge the inappropriate behaviour and explain how the comments are not in line with organisational policy.

  D. Report the comments to my line manager. It is their responsibility to deal with this kind of issue.

The correct answer to this question is:

Immediately challenge the inappropriate behaviour and explain how the comments are not in line with organisational policy.

No form of bullying, harassment or inappropriate comments is tolerated in the Fire Service. It is your responsibility to proactively challenge them. How do we know this if we are not already serving in the Fire

Service? The simple answer is that if you learn and understand the PQAs, then you will be able to answer the question.

Here is an extract from the PQA of Commitment to Diversity and Integrity:

"Proactively challenges unacceptable behaviour inconsistent with Fire & Rescue Service values, stating own and organisation's position clearly (e.g. when over-hearing a colleague use inappropriate language)."

Unless you have read the PQAs, you could be mistaken for believing That the correct answer is D. I cannot stress enough how important your success depends on your understanding and knowledge of the PQA's.

Whilst not every question during this test will depend on your knowledge of the PQAs, a number of them will. Learn them, absorb them, and understand them!

Now take a look at the practice questions on the following pages. You have 35 minutes in which to answer the 30 questions. The answers and full explanations are provided at the end of the test section.

Situational Awareness and Problem Solving Test 1

1. A work colleague in the Fire Service has been absent due to sickness and she has missed an important operational incident debrief that has highlighted a number of important change to procedures. What would you do?

A) Immediately explain to her what the changes are and clarify that she fully understands them.

b) Inform your line manager of her absence so that he can tell her what they are.

C) Do nothing. She will probably find out about the changes through other work colleagues or whilst she is on the job.

D) Wait until tea break before you inform her. There'll be more time then to explain what the changes are.

2. Whilst attending a Road Traffic Collision as a firefighter, you notice a work colleague using an item of equipment that you are not familiar with. What would you do?

A) Allow them to carry on using the item of equipment as they probably know how to use it correctly. You are not expected to know how everything works.

B) Approach the firefighter and ask them if you can have a go with the equipment. It would be a good idea to start using the equipment so that I become familiar with it, and what better time than to start than right now.

C) Wait until I get back to the station, then familiarise myself with the equipment making sure that I fully read the operational training manual.

D) Wait until I get back to the station, then get a colleague to show me how to use it after a well-earned tea break.

3. Firefighters are often required to enter people's homes in order to carry out home fire safety checks and to offer fire safety advice when requested. Whilst attending someone's home to fit a smoke alarm, they offer you £50 as a thank you for the work that you have done. What would you do?

A) Thank them for the money, put it in my pocket, and leave a happy person.

B) Thank them for the money, put it in my pocket, and share it with the rest of the watch when I get back to the fire station.

C) Thank them for their kind offer but explain that you are unable to accept gifts of this nature.

D) Walk away and ignore them.

4. During an operational incident the officer-in-charge gives you instructions to immediately stop what you are doing and request more resources via the control centre, due to the fire spreading rapidly. Once you have received the instructions, what would you do?

A) Finish off the job that I am doing before contacting the control centre to request more resources.

B) Immediately stop what I am doing if safe to do so before contacting the control centre to request more resources. Once I have requested the resources, and confirmed that the control centre fully understands my request, I will then inform the officer-in-charge that the message has been sent and that the resources are on their way. I would then return to my previous task.

C) Because I am already involved in another task, I will pass the message onto another firefighter so that he can request the resources. Team work is an important aspect of our job.

D) Immediately stop what I am doing if safe to do so before contacting the control centre to request more resources. Once I have requested the resources, and confirmed that the control centre fully understands my request, I will then go back to what I was doing before.

5. Whilst attending a fire in a block of flats, which of the following tasks would you carry out first?

A) Check your equipment before using it so that it is safe.

B) Fight the fire.

C) Evacuate the people inside the burning building.

D) Contact the control centre and ask for more resources.

6. Whilst attending a Road Traffic Collision (RTC) involving three people trapped inside a car, which of the following tasks would you carry out second?

A) Make the car safe and stable before working on it.

B) Carry out an immediate assessment of all the casualties in the car to ascertain their injuries and to make sure they are breathing.

C) Get the hydraulic rescue equipment ready so that we can extricate the casualties.

D) Place a neck brace on each of the casualties to prevent any further damage or injury.

7. You are attending a fire inside a house, searching for casualties. When you entered the building, you had 180 bars of pressure inside your cylinder. How often would you check your breathing apparatus cylinder gauge to see how much air you have left?

A) I would check the gauge every 5 minutes.

B) I would check the gauge regularly and periodically.

C) I would look at the gauge all of the time.

D) I would look at the gauge when my gut instinct told me to do so.

8. During a community fire safety visit to a local school, you notice that a number of the fire doors are wedged open illegally. What do you do?

A) Ignore it for the time being. You are at the school on a community fire safety visit and it would be inappropriate to say anything there and then.

B) Report the situation to the local Fire Safety Officer when you return to the station.

C) Inform the school Head teacher that he/she must remove the wedges immediately.

D) Inform the school Head teacher that he/she must remove the wedges immediately and explain why the fire doors must not be wedged open. In addition to this I would inform the local Fire Safety Officer upon returning to the station so that he/she could carry out an inspection of the school.

9. You are attending an incident that involves a fire in a warehouse. You notice that the fire is starting to spread to a neighbouring building. What would you do?

A) Quickly run over to where the fire is spreading and shout for help.

B) Stay calm, carry out an assessment of the situation, write down what I see and then pass all details on to my line manager so he can decide what to do next.

C) Immediately inform my line manager of the situation and start to tackle the fire in order to prevent it from spreading any further, in line with operational procedures and training.

D) Inform my line manager and then wait for back up to arrive before taking any action.

10. Whilst serving as a firefighter at your local station, you become concerned that the standard of operational training has been dropping over the last few months. What do you do?

A) Provide feedback to the line manager on how you believe the training could be improved in order to improve service delivery.

B) At the end of the day, any issues surrounding training standards are down to the line manager. It is up to them to sort it out and if they can't recognise there's a problem, then that's not my problem.

C) Apply for promotion so that you can be in charge of training and therefore improve the standards.

D) Discuss your concerns with the other members of the watch. If they agree with you, then inform the line manager.

11. You are called to a fire in a factory. As you turn the corner in the fire engine, you notice a gang of youths running away. You suspect that they may have started the fire deliberately. What would you do?

A) Any issues relating to who started the fire are not your concern. You are there to fight the fire and that is what you will do.

B) Suggest to the line manager that half of the team tackle the fire whilst the other half run after the youths.

C) Tackle the fire and request the attendance of the Police so that they can investigate this issue.

D) Put the fire out first and then drive around in the fire engine looking for the youths.

12. You are attending an incident where a child has fallen into a deep pond and he is struggling to stay afloat. As a firefighter you must not enter water without a buoyancy aid and at this incident you do not have one. What would you do?

A) I would take my clothes off to prevent myself from sinking and swim in after the boy. I am strong swimmer and would be able to rescue him.

B) I would throw the boy a rope and tell him to grab it. Then I would try to pull him to the side with my colleagues.

C) I would take my clothes off and go into the water up to waste height only with a rope securely tied around my waste. This way I would be able to rescue him without endangering myself.

D) I am not permitted to enter the water without a buoyancy aid; therefore, I am powerless to help the boy.

13. A firefighter work colleague, who is from a different ethnic background to yourself, asks you if you would cover part of their shift whilst they pray. What would you do?

A) This has got nothing to do with work and therefore they should not be allowed time to pray. I would not cover their shift.

B) I would refuse.

C) I would be happy to cover part of their shift if they promised to pay back the time at a later date.

D) I would be happy to cover part of their shift as I understand that, as part of their religious beliefs, they need time to pray.

14. Whilst fitting a smoke alarm in someone's home you notice a firefighter take some money from a sideboard cabinet that belongs to the household owner. What would you do?

A. Tell them to put the money back and then inform your line manager.

B. Tell them to put the money back and then get them to promise that they will never do that sort of thing again.

C. Ignore it.

D. Tell them to put the money back and then inform the household owner.

15. Whilst in the locker room you notice a pornographic magazine on the window ledge. What would you do?

A) Pick it up and read it.

B) Shake your head and say to yourself whoever brought that into work should be ashamed of themselves.

C) Immediately remove the magazine, place it in the nearest bin and then inform my line manager.

D) Ask around the station if anyone knows who it belongs to and then ask them to put it away in their locker.

16. During a watch meeting your line manager is explaining a number of changes that are being introduced to the working day. These changes will mean that you and your work colleagues will need to carry out more Community Fire Safety visits. The majority of other members of the watch start to make their objections to the changes heard. What would you do?

A) Join in with the objections. Why change things when everything is going OK as it is?

B) Keep your head down. Whilst you don't agree with the changes you don't want to get into trouble for raising your concerns.

C) Accept the changes yourself. It doesn't matter what the others think. After all, they are entitled to their own opinion!

D) Accept the changes. Change is part of Fire Service life. I would also try and explain the benefit of the changes to those who are sceptical.

17. You wake up one morning and start to get ready for work. All of a sudden you start to feel ill and uneasy. Whilst driving to work your eyes become slightly blurred, but you are just about OK to drive. When you arrive at work you still feel slightly ill. What would you do?

A) Inform your line manager about how you feel.

B) Battle through it. You are a firefighter and you have a responsibility to be ready for an emergency.

C) Take headache tablets and monitor the situation. If you feel bad during the afternoon then you will consider booking sick.

D) Ask a work colleague if you can ride the turntable ladder instead of the fire engine. The turntable ladder very rarely goes out so you will have time to recuperate and feel better.

18. Your line manager has asked you to clean the appliance bay floor 5 minutes before you are due to go off duty. You realise that this will take you 10 minutes to do the job professionally. What would you do?

A) Carry out the task as requested professionally, even though it will mean that you have to stay behind at work for an additional 5 minutes.

B) Inform your manager that you are going off duty in 5 minutes time and ask her if there is anyone else who can do the task.

C) Carry out the task to a slightly lesser standard, therefore finishing your shift on time.

D) Politely refuse to carry out the task. After all, it will take you 5 minutes to get your fire kit off the fire engine and hand over to the oncoming watch.

19. During an appraisal with your line manager, she raises a number of concerns regarding your performance at work. She states that she feels you are not getting involved in community safety projects enough and that she wants you to make improvements in this area. What would you do?

A) Do as she tells me. I might not agree with her comments, but she is the boss at the end of the day.

B) Apologise if this is the case and immediately take steps to improve in this area by volunteering to become more involved. I would also ask for regular feedback on any future performance.

C) I would ask to see evidence of where I am supposed to be failing. Without proof I cannot make any improvements.

D) I would tell her that whilst community safety is an important aspect for Fire Service life, the most important thing is being ready to attend operational incidents and the training that goes with that. You will try and get more involved in the future, but operational readiness must always come first.

20. You are attending a fire in a terraced house and a crowd has gathered outside. The house involved in the fire is the home of man who is registered as a sex offender. The crowd are becoming more vocal and are starting to shout words of abuse at the home owner. What would you do?

A) It is understandable that the crowd feel this way and therefore I would allow the shouting to continue; he is getting what he deserves at the end of the day.

B) I would approach the crowd and threaten them with Police action if they do not cease the abuse. I would tell them that I understand how they feel, but they need to be quiet whilst you tackle the blaze.

C) I would inform my line manager so that he could make a decision on what to do next.

D) I would ask the crowd to keep back and create a cordon a safe distance away from the scene. I would then inform my line manager about the situation and request the attendance of the Police.

21. You are sat around the mess table having a cup of tea with the rest of the watch. There's a bit of banter going on and one of the more senior firefighters is making fun out of the new probationary firefighter. The new firefighter appears to be slightly upset by the comments but doesn't say anything. What would you do?

A) I would intervene and say that I didn't think the comments were appropriate. Even though the firefighter is new, that doesn't mean he should be the centre of any harmful jokes or comments.

B) Banter is all part and parcel of Fire Service life. Firefighters work together in sometimes difficult and stressful situations and they would do anything for each other. A bit of banter is good for morale and if the new probationary firefighter is going to fit in, then he will need to get used to it.

C) I would leave the room and go and inform my line manager of the comments.

D) I would probably join in with the banter.

22. You are carrying out a home fire safety visit in a family's home who are from the Muslim community. During your visit, the lady stops you and says that she is struggling to understand what you are saying. What would you do?

A) Explain politely that she will have to listen more carefully as you do not speak her language.

B) Ask another member of her family to interpret, even if they too are struggling to understand.

C) Not waste any more of their time and politely leave the house. It's pointless talking to them about Fire Safety if they don't understand what you are saying.

D) Apologise, and tell them that you will return as soon as possible with an interpreter, and also with some Fire Safety leaflets that are in their native language. I believe it is important that they understand the message so that they are safe.

23. You have been serving as a firefighter for six years and are a respected member of your watch. Your line manager approaches you and asks you to take the new probationary firefighter under your wing. You start talking to him, whilst showing him around the station, and he confides in you that he is gay. He tells you that he is worried what the other members of the watch will say, and asks for your advice. What would you do?

A) I would tell him that his sexual orientation is not a problem and makes no different to how he will be treated at work. If he does have any problems, then he can come to me or the line manager immediately for support and advice.

B) I would tell him that, because we all sleep in the same room together at night, it would be best if he kept his secret to himself. The other members of the watch might be offended. Providing that he doesn't make any advances on me, and keeps himself to himself, then it shouldn't be a problem.

C) I would immediately tell the line manager. We don't want gay firefighters on the watch.

D) I would tell him that he will probably get a bit of stick from the other members of the watch, but that means that they will like him and that he'll be popular.

24. You are attending a chemical incident at a factory where a barrel containing a suspected dangerous substance is leaking. You are the only fire engine in attendance at the scene. The Chemical Incident Unit (ICU), which contains all the necessary protective equipment to deal with the incident, is 8 minutes away. You notice that the leak from the barrel is intensifying. What would you do?

A) I would run over to the barrel and try and seal it.

B) I don't know what I would do.

C) I would clear the area of any people, create a safe cordon, and then wait for the ICU to arrive. I would not go anywhere near the barrel until I was wearing the appropriate personal protective equipment.

D) I would clear the area of any people, create a safe cordon, and the walk carefully up to the barrel with a pen and paper. I would then take down any safety advice or information that was on the barrel so that I could hand it over to the officer-in-charge of the ICU when he arrives. This would mean that the barrel could then be sealed off quickly using the correct equipment, as per the advice contained on the barrel.

25. Who would you help first?

A) A man locked out of his house during the day.

B) A woman locked out of her house during the day.

C) A family from Poland living the UK who do not have a smoke alarm.

D) A cat up a tree.

26. You are attending a fire in a block of flats. What would you do first?

A) Activate the fire alarm.

B) Fight the fire.

C) Ventilate the property to clear the smoke.

D) Get everyone out of the building.

27. When would you risk your life a lot, in a highly calculated manner?

A) During a training session.

B) To rescue a pet that had been left inside a burning building.

C) To save property.

D) To protect saveable lives.

28. When would you ask permission from your line manager before you took action?

A) To fight a fire that had started to spread to an adjacent building.

B) To rescue a work colleague who had become trapped under a pile of bricks and debris.

C) To stabilise a car during a Road Traffic Collision before entering it to free the casualty.

D) To break down a door to a building where the fire alarm was sounding.

29. Part of your role as a firefighter is to provide advice to local businesses in relation to Fire Safety. Whilst attending an incident at an office block, which resulted in a false alarm, what would you advise the occupiers?

A) To put up Fire Safety posters in their offices.

B) To clean the fire alarm weekly so that it doesn't go off as often.

C) That they have a legal duty to carry out a risk assessment in the workplace, inform all staff of its findings, and to also provide suitable training.

D) To test the smoke alarm battery once a month.

30. Whilst attending an incident you are confronted by a gang of youths who start throwing stones at your fire engine. What would you do?

A) Pick up the stones and throw them back. It's important that we send a message to these people that we will not tolerate this kind of action.

B) Stay calm and ignore them. We have a job to do.

C) Stay calm, request the immediate attendance of the Police and withdraw from the incident.

D) Fight back by unleashing the fire hose on them.

Situational Awareness and Problem Solving – Answers to Test 1

The answers to the following questions include details of personal experiences from author Richard McMunn.

1. A. Immediately explain to her what the changes are and clarify that she fully understands them.

This question relates to the PQA of openness to change:

"Demonstrates an understanding of the need for change within the Fire and Rescue Service (e.g. explains the reasons for new working practices to colleagues absent from briefings)."

It is important that she is informed immediately about the changes. If you were to select answer D, then there is a possibility that you could get turned out to an incident before tea break and your colleague would not be fully informed of the changes, and this could be dangerous.

2. C. Wait until I get back to the station, then familiarise myself with the equipment making sure that I fully read the operational training manual.

To start using the item of equipment there and then, on the job, would be dangerous. After all, you are attending a Road Traffic Collision where the risk factors are far higher than normal. Therefore, the most sensible option would be to wait until you return to station before familiarising yourself with the equipment. It is important that, as a firefighter, you are familiar with all items of equipment on your fire engine. It is also important that you read any operational instructions or training notes that accompany items of operational equipment.

3. C. Thank them for their kind offer but explain that you are unable to accept gifts of this nature.

The majority of Fire and Rescue Services do not allow firefighters to accept personal gifts from members of the public. In this case, the correct answer would be C, to thank them for their kind offer but explain that you are unable to accept the gift. However, many Fire and Rescue Services do allow firefighters to accept donations for their charity, which is called the Fire Services National Benevolent Fund. In cases where money is accepted as a charity donation, you would need to issue a receipt to the individual who has donated the money.

4. B. Immediately stop what I am doing if safe to do so before contacting the control centre to request more resources.

Once I have requested the resources, and confirmed that the control centre fully understands my request, I will then inform the officer-in-charge that the message has been sent and that the resources are on their way. I would then return to my previous task.

Effective communication is crucial to the safety of all firefighters. Whilst attending operational incidents it is important that you listen carefully to all instructions, do what you are told, and also check/confirm that any information passed or received is accurate.

You will see during the above correct answer that the firefighter not only follows the instructions of his or her officer-in-charge, but they also confirm to see that their message has been understood by the control centre. Finally, they will inform the officer-in-charge that the message has been sent.

During an operational incident there are many different things going on at any one time. Therefore, there is a strong possibility that things can get forgotten. This is why it is important to not only check for understanding, but to also confirm that messages have been sent.

If you read and absorb the PQA's, you will notice that the PQA of effective communication states the following:

"Checks understanding to ensure all messages received and sent are understood correctly."

5. C. Evacuate the people inside the burning building.

During any incident of this type it is important that you evacuate the people inside the burning building. If the building has a fire alarm, and it is not already sounding, then you should activate it immediately. This will alert any people inside the building who are not already aware of the fire, so that they can start to make their way out. Whilst it is important to fight the fire and save the building, the safety of you, your colleagues, and the people inside the building is paramount.

6. MA. Make the car safe and stable before working on it.

This is quite a difficult question to answer, especially if you have no experience of how to deal with Road Traffic Collisions! However, as with all of the questions, try to think about the situation logically.

The question asks you to identify the second task that you would carry out in this scenario. The first, and most obvious task, is to carry out an immediate assessment of all the casualties in the car in order to ascertain their injuries, and to also make sure they are breathing. If they are breathing, and their injuries are not life threatening, then you will have more time in which to deal with the situation. However, if they are not breathing, then you would need to carry out the correct procedures and make efforts to revive them.

The danger with this type of incident is that firefighters, and other members of the emergency services, can inflict further injury to the casualties by clambering all over the vehicle. If a casualty has injuries, then a firefighter working inside the vehicle could exacerbate or intensify the injury. Therefore, before any further work is carried out on, to, or inside the vehicle, it must be made safe and stable. Therefore, the correct answer is A, make the car safe and stable before working on it.

7.B. I would check the gauge regularly and periodically.

During this type of scenario is it is very important that you regularly check the contents of your breathing apparatus cylinder. There are many different factors that can determine the quantity of air that you breathe, such as:

- Your own personal fitness levels.

- The type and intensity of the task that you are carrying out whilst wearing the breathing apparatus. For example, you will use your air up far quicker if you are carrying out a task such as lifting or moving heavy equipment.

- The intensity of the fire or the heat.

- How calm you remain whilst wearing the breathing apparatus set. Therefore, due to the above factors, it is crucial that you check your problems with your set.

8. D. Inform the school Head teacher that he/she must remove the wedges immediately and explain why the fire doors must not be wedged open.

In addition to this I would inform the local Fire Safety Officer upon returning to the station so that he/she could carry out an inspection of the school.

As a firefighter you will attend many different buildings, not just during operational incidents, but also during community fire safety and familiarisation visits. I guarantee that during many of these visits you will notice that some of the fire doors are illegally wedged open. Many people wedge open fire doors for reasons such as:

- The doors are used frequently and therefore to keep opening them becomes a hindrance.

- So that boxes and furniture etc can be moved through them quickly.

- So that fresh air can circulate through the building during hot weather.

The simple fact is, a fire door is there for a purpose, and that purpose is to protect the occupants from becoming trapped inside a building during a fire, and also to prevent the spread of fire. It is illegal to wedge open a fire door and therefore you must take action to remove the wedge or other obstacle immediately. It is also important to explain to the responsible person for the building why it is illegal to wedge open fire doors. You should also follow up your actions by informing the local Fire Safety Officer so that he/she can carry out a visit at the building. After all, if they are wedging open fire doors, what else are they doing that could be putting the occupants in danger?

9. C. Immediately inform my line manager of the situation and start to tackle the fire in order to prevent it from spreading any further, in line with operational procedures and training.

In this type of situation immediate action is vital. I have been to many different fires of this nature where the fire takes hold on adjacent buildings and the consequences can be severe. As a firefighter you will need to be vigilant and look out for the fire spreading to adjacent or nearby buildings. If you notice the fire spreading, immediately inform your supervisor and take action to prevent the fire from spreading in accordance with your training and operational procedures.

10. A. Provide feedback to the line manager on how you believe the training could be improved in order to improve service delivery.

If you have read the PQA of commitment to excellence, then you will be able to answer this question with relative ease. Part of the PQA states:

"Continually looks to improve standards of working and offers suggestions as necessary (e.g. provides feedback concerning new or existing work practices to influence change or improve service delivery)."

In the Fire Service, if you have any suggestions as to how service delivery can be improved, then you should say so!

11. C. Tackle the fire and request the attendance of the Police so that they can investigate this issue.

As tempting as it may seem, it is not your place to start running after alleged arsonists! Not only will you be putting yourself in danger, but you could also land yourself in serious trouble with the Fire Service and

the Police. It is the responsibility of the Police to assist in matters of this nature; your immediate concern is to tackle the fire. During incidents of this nature your line manager would request, through the control centre, the attendance of the Police so that they can search for the youths.

12. B. I would throw the boy a rope and tell him to grab it. Then I would try to pull him to the side with my colleagues.

This type of scenario is extremely rare; however, it has happened before, and it will happen again. There is much debate as to what a person, who is a member of the emergency services, should do in this type of situation.

Personally, if I were a firefighter, I would go in after the boy. I am a very strong swimmer and I would feel confident that I could rescue him. I could not live with myself if I knew that the boy had drowned because I followed procedures and did not go in after him, simply because I did not have a buoyancy aid. However, during this book I am teaching you the right way to do things, and therefore the correct answer is B. The reason why procedures prevent you from going in after the boy is simple:

Let's assume that you take your clothes off and go in the pond to rescue the boy. What happens if you get into trouble yourself? What happens if

the rope that you have tied around your waste suddenly becomes snagged under a tree that is submerged underneath the water? Hopefully you can start to realise now why there are strict procedures in place to protect you and your work colleagues.

13. D. I would be happy to cover part of their shift as I understand that, as part of their religious beliefs, they need time to pray.

Society is diverse and rich in culture. If society is diverse and rich in culture, then so should the workplace. During your time in the Fire Service you will be working with people of different ages, different backgrounds, different religious beliefs, different gender and different sexual orientation.

It is important that you feel comfortable with working alongside a variety of different people and appreciate the benefits that it can bring. It would be a very boring place if we were all one colour, one age and one sex!

Understanding and being accommodating of people's needs is an important part of the firefighter's role. If you read the PQA of Commitment to Diversity and Integrity, it states:

Is concerned to treat people fairly and ethically (e.g. completes work according to same high standards regardless of individual differences)

Recognises the importance of an awareness of the community and understands its needs (e.g. is aware and respectful of differing cultures and backgrounds)

Recognises and has respect for others' backgrounds, views, values and beliefs (including religious beliefs)

If you are not prepared to demonstrate a commitment to diversity and integrity, then this job isn't for you.

14. A. Tell them to put the money back and then inform your line manager.

There is absolutely no room for thieves in the Fire Service. You are entrusted to go into people's homes on a regular basis, and therefore you are expected to abide by protocol, rules and procedures. You must never take anything that belongs to another person. In this instance it is important that you inform your line manager so that they can instigate discipline procedures and inform the Police if necessary.

If you read the PQA's carefully, you will notice that the PQA for commitment to diversity and integrity states:

"Is honest when working with others and accepts accountability for own actions (e.g. takes responsibility for own mistakes; respects the need for confidentiality; is trusted to enter others' homes)."

15. C. Immediately remove the magazine, place it in the nearest bin and then inform my line manager.

Modern day Fire Stations are public places. They are also places for both men and women. Therefore, any magazines or material that may be deemed offensive are not tolerated and should be removed. In this case, answer C is correct.

16. D. Accept the changes. Change is part of Fire Service life. I would also try and explain the benefit of the changes to those who are sceptical.

The PQA of openness to change was introduced a few years ago for one simple reason – many people in the Fire Service did not accept change easily. Having personally served as a Watch Manager, and a Station Man- ager in charge of a number of Fire Stations, I can vouch for this. Change within any organisation can be uncomfortable; however, change can be

a positive thing and it can improve the way an organisation delivers its service. In the case of the Fire Service, change is essential.

The PQA states:

- Demonstrates an understanding of the need for change within the Fire and Rescue Service (e.g. explains the reasons for new working practices to colleagues absent from briefings)

- Aware of the impact of changes to the Fire and Rescue Service on their role (e.g. understands changes to working practices)

- Accepts change both within the Fire and Rescue Service and in their own role (e.g. willingly participates in community fire safety activities)

- Identifies ways, both within the Fire and Rescue Service and the local community, of supporting change and takes action to support it.

17. A. Inform your line manager about how you feel.

Firefighters are caring people and naturally they want to work. I have myself been on duty as a firefighter and started to feel ill. The last thing I wanted to do was book off sick! However, the safety of yourself, your work colleagues and the members of public whom you are serving, comes first. Therefore, the correct answer is to inform your line manager, or even book off sick.

The last thing you want to do is collapse whilst you are the top of a ladder fighting a fire!

18. A. Carry out the task as requested professionally, even though it will mean that you have to stay behind at work for an additional 5 minutes.

Staying behind at work for a few minutes isn't going to hurt. Firefighters enjoy good working conditions and it is all about give and take. The correct answer is that you should stay behind to complete the task professionally. The PQA for commitment to excellence states:

"Adopts a conscientious approach to work (e.g. checks work to ensure all tasks completed correctly and with due attention to detail; maintains levels of personal fitness)."

19. B. Apologise if this is the case and immediately take steps to improve in this area by volunteering to become more involved. I would also ask for regular feedback on any future performance.

The PQA for commitment to development states:

"Proactively reviews own performance using a variety of sources

including seeking feedback from others."

Being able to take constructive criticism is an important aspect of the firefighter's role. You will receive regular appraisals whilst at work and it is vital that you take on board the comments. This will allow you to continually improve as a firefighter. Community fire safety is an extremely important part of your job too. You must be willing to undertake this type of work in order to make the community a safer place to live. Community fire safety work is just as important as attending incidents.

> 20. D. I would ask the crowd to keep back and create a cordon a safe distance away from the scene. I would then inform my line manager about the situation and request the attendance of the Police.

Even though the home owner is a registered sex offender, this does not make the abuse acceptable. As a firefighter you should never get involved, or drawn into, situations like this. Your job is to keep yourself, your work colleagues and the members of the public safe at all times. By creating a cordon away from the incident, you will be allowing yourself some breathing space whilst you await the arrival of the Police. Incidents of this nature are the responsibility of the Police and therefore their attendance should be requested immediately.

> 21. A. I would intervene and say that I didn't think the comments were appropriate. Even though the firefighter is new, that doesn't mean he should be the centre of any harmful jokes or comments.

I've been in this type of situation myself as a probationary firefighter and jokes, whilst no harm intended, can sometimes be inappropriate and hurtful. If you have taken the time to read and learn the PQAs, you will be aware that the commitment to diversity and integrity states:

"Proactively challenges unacceptable behaviour inconsistent with Fire & Rescue Service values, stating own and organisation's position clearly (e.g. when over-hearing a colleague use inappropriate language)."

The correct answer is that you must have the confidence to challenge comments that are inappropriate. In this case the probationary firefighter would probably not have the confidence to say that the comments were hurtful.

22. D. Apologise, and tell them that you will return as soon as possible with an interpreter, and also with some Fire Safety leaflets that are in their native language. I believe it is important that they understand the message so that they are safe.

I have been in this situation before, where a member of the community is struggling to understand what I am saying. In the Fire Service that I served in, Kent Fire and Rescue Service, we were fortunate enough to have an interpreter who we could call upon in situations such as these. Whatever you do, it is crucial that every member of the community receives the same treatment and service. Sometimes that will mean having to go that extra mile to help them, and to also make sure they fully understand the Fire Safety message that you are trying to put across.

The PQA of commitment to diversity and integrity states:

"Recognises the importance of an awareness of the community and understands its needs (e.g. is aware and respectful of differing cultures and backgrounds)."

23. A. I would tell him that his sexual orientation is not a problem and makes no different to how he will be treated at work. If he does have any problems, then he can come to me or the line manager immediately for support and advice.

The Fire Service has, until recently, had quite a 'macho' image. In the days gone by, if you were gay or lesbian, then you probably wouldn't feel comfortable about 'coming out' to your watch. However, things are now changing in the Fire Service, and rightly so. If you are homophobic, racist or a bully, then the Fire Service is not the job for you. Everybody, regardless of their sexual orientation, age, gender, disability or racial background, should feel comfortable at work.

The PQA of commitment to diversity and integrity carries a far higher 'weight' during the firefighter selection process than the remainder of the PQAs. Therefore, it is important that you not only understand it, but also genuinely believe in it.

The PQA states:

"Maintains an open approach with others, taking account of, and accepting, individual differences such as age, ethnicity, gender,

religious beliefs, social background, disability, sexual orientation and physical appearance."

24. C. I would clear the area of any people, create a safe cordon and then wait for the ICU to arrive. I would not go anywhere near the barrel until I was wearing the appropriate personal protective equipment.

Whatever you do during your career as a firefighter, always be safe. In this situation, it is important that you clear the area of any people, create a cordon and then wait for the specialist vehicle to arrive. Even if the leak intensifies further, you must wait for the ICU to arrive. It simply is not worth risking your lungs for a barrel full of chemicals! Even if you suspect that the barrel is harmless, always be on the side of caution.

Before you approach anything of this nature, you must always wear a Gas Tight Suit (GTS) and breathing apparatus, or some other form of safety clothing that is endorsed by your Fire Service.

25. C. A family from Poland living the UK who do not have a smoke alarm.

Did you choose the correct answer? Not many people do! Most people choose either the cat up the tree, or the woman locked out of her home.

The people who are most at risk are the family from Poland, simply because they are in a different country to their own, and they also do not have a smoke alarm. The man and woman, who are locked out of their homes, can call a lock smith. The modern-day Fire Service very rarely attends incidents of this nature anymore, unless the person locked out is vulnerable in some way. With regards to the cat up the tree, it is often the case that the cat will find its own way down. If the Fire Service do attend and try to rescue it, they can be at high risk because the cat will not normally sit still and wait to be rescued!

26. A. Activate the fire alarm.

This question is quite a difficult one to answer, unless you think about it logically. Most people choose either to evacuate the building, or fight the fire. The reason why 'A' is the correct is as follows:

If the fire alarm is not yet sounding, then it must be activated immediately. This will make everyone in the building aware that there is a fire.

Do not assume at any incident that, just because there is a fire, the occupants will be aware of its existence. A fire is silent, which is why people who do not have a smoke alarm, are far more likely to die in a fire than those who do have one that is working.

Unless you are aware of the layout of the building, you will have no idea how many homes are within the block of flats. Therefore, making everyone aware of the fire and the need to evacuate becomes harder. Blocks of flats are often constructed using dense concrete walls and any form of shouting is unlikely to be heard by the occupants. That is why buildings of this nature are normally always fitted with an appropriate fire alarm system. Make sure it is activated immediately in incidents of this nature.

27. D. To protect saveable lives.

The Fire Service has a healthy attitude towards 'safety'. Read and absorb the following:

"We may risk our lives a lot, in a highly calculated manner, to protect saveable lives. We may risk our lives a little, in a highly controlled manner, to protect saveable property. We will not risk our lives at all for lives or property that are already lost."

28. D. To break down a door to a building where the fire alarm was sounding.

When answering this type of question, apply a level of logical thinking. Let's take a look at each one individually:

v. To fight a fire that had started to spread to an adjacent building.

During this type of incident every second counts. You must act quickly. If you don't, the fire will take a hold on the adjacent building. Therefore, finding your line manager to ask him/her if it's OK for you to fight the fire that is quickly spreading to the adjacent building is not the right option! You must think on your feet in order to save the building.

vi. To rescue a work colleague who had become trapped under a pile of bricks and debris.

Again, it is obvious what your line manager will say when you ask her:

"Is it OK if I rescue Dave who is trapped under that rubble of bricks?"

As a firefighter, you will be fully trained to deal with incidents of this nature.

vii. To stabilise a car during a Road Traffic Collision before entering it to free the casualty.

Once again, as a firefighter, you will be fully trained in RTC procedures, and therefore you will act as a matter of course to stabilise the vehicle before entering it.

viii. To break down a door to a building where the fire alarm was sounding.

Although a fire alarm is sounding in a building, it does not necessarily mean there is a fire. How many times have you been in a building, premise, or other establishment when the fire alarm has sounded? How many times has the fire alarm gone off, and there has been an actual fire? Very few I'm sure. Over 90% of fire alarm activations end up being a false alarm, therefore, you should always ask permission from your line manager before causing considerable damage to a property by breaking down the door when there are no signs of fire or smoke.

29. C. That they have a legal duty to carry out a risk assessment in the workplace, inform all staff of its findings, and to also provide suitable training.

Every business has a responsibility to carry out a risk assessment, report the findings to its employees, and to also provide suitable training.

30. C. Stay calm, request the immediate attendance of the Police and withdraw from the incident.

In this kind of situation, you must never fight back. You should remain calm, immediately request the attendance of the Police and withdraw from the incident. Your life and the lives of your colleagues should never be placed under unnecessary threat.

Tips for Passing the Situational Awareness and Problem Solving Test

- Read the question quickly but carefully. Remember that you are being assessed in the areas of 'situational awareness' and 'problem solving'.

- Remember that firefighters must work safely. Think about your responses carefully. If one of the choices sounds dangerous then the likelihood is that it is the wrong answer.

- Learn the personal qualities and attributes (PQAs) of a firefighter before you take the tests. This will give you a good understanding of what the firefighter's role entails. Once you understand the PQA's, many of the answers will jump out at you.

Chapter 5
National Firefighter
Questionnaire

During the firefighter selection process, you will be required to complete a questionnaire. The purpose of this questionnaire is to determine your attitude, motivations and opinions in relation to situations centred on the Personal Qualities and Attributes.

There are no right or wrong answers to the questions, but the questionnaire should be taken seriously as it will be used to determine whether or not your application is successful. So, it is very important that you do not rush through it, which many candidates seem to do. For some reason, they don't believe that it carries much weight, when in fact it does. My advice to you is simple:

- Learn the PQAs thoroughly. If you learn and understand them, the questionnaire will be far easier to complete.

- Be truthful. It is important that you answer the questions honestly.

- Do not rush the questionnaire. There is normally no time limit, so the pressure is off!

During the questionnaire there are approximately 120 – 130 questions to answer. As you progress through it, you will notice that some of the questions repeat themselves, albeit they are asked in a different manner. Your answers should be as consistent as possible.

> *The following example responses are from the author, Richard McMunn.*

Here's an example:

1. It is true that I embrace change at every opportunity

☐   Strongly agree

☐   Agree

☐   Neither agree or disagree

☐   Disagree

☐   Strongly disagree

For me personally, I would answer this question 'strongly agree'. I understand that change within the Fire Service is important and it is vital that I embrace it – read the PQA for 'openness to change'.

And now here's the same question, posed in a different manner:

2. I tend to not embrace change and see no need for it

☐   Strongly agree

☐   Agree

☐   Neither agree or disagree

☐   Disagree

☐   Strongly disagree

I would respond to this question with 'Strongly Disagree'. Because I have already stated in Question 1 that I embrace change, it is important that I am consistent throughout the questionnaire. Therefore, I strongly disagree that I tend not to embrace change and see no need for it.

I appreciate that the questionnaire is confusing, which is why I recommend you take your time when completing it. Use up all of the time you have available, don't rush and thoroughly learn the PQA's. These will give you an indication as to the type of responses the Fire Service is looking for.

Time and time again I get asked the question "should I respond with 'strongly agree/disagree, or simply agree/disagree". This is a very good question!

My advice is this:

There are a number of PQAs that are extremely important. Openness to change is one of them, commitment to diversity and integrity is another.

You will need to decide yourself how strongly you either agree or disagree about certain questions. You may even decide to respond with 'neither agree or disagree' to some questions depending on your views or opinions.

At the end of the test that follows in this section of the guide, I have provided you with examples of how I would personally respond to the questions. This will give you an insight into my feelings towards specific situations.

I have now provided you with 50 sample questions to assist you. Take your time to work through them carefully. There is no time limit.

Personality Questionnaire Test

1. I tend to embrace change at work.

   ☐ Strongly agree

   ☐ Agree

   ☐ Neither agree or disagree

   ☐ Disagree

   ☐ Strongly disagree

2. I would take just as much care and attention when mopping the fire station floor as I would be servicing my breathing apparatus set.

   ☐ Strongly agree

   ☐ Agree

   ☐ Neither agree or disagree

   ☐ Disagree

   ☐ Strongly disagree

3. I believe it is acceptable for people to get angry every now and again.

   ☐ Strongly agree

   ☐ Agree

   ☐ Neither agree or disagree

   ☐ Disagree

   ☐ Strongly disagree

4. Different cultures of people in the community are not beneficial to society.

   ☐ Strongly agree

   ☐ Agree

☐ Neither agree or disagree

☐ Disagree

☐ Strongly disagree

5. If I witnessed a work colleague being bullied by another employee I would leave them both to sort it out themselves. Getting involved would probably make it worse.

☐ Strongly agree

☐ Agree

☐ Neither agree or disagree

☐ Disagree

☐ Strongly disagree

6. If I made a mistake I would own up to it straight away.

☐ Strongly agree

☐ Agree

☐ Neither agree or disagree

☐ Disagree

☐ Strongly disagree

7. I have been known on occasions to panic and lose control.

☐ Strongly agree

☐ Agree

☐ Neither agree or disagree

☐ Disagree

☐ Strongly disagree

8. With regards to change, I believe that you shouldn't fix things if they are not broken.

☐ Strongly agree

☐ Agree

☐ Neither agree or disagree

☐ Disagree

☐ Strongly disagree

9. I find it easy to concentrate on tasks, despite external distractions.

☐ Strongly agree

☐ Agree

☐ Neither agree or disagree

☐ Disagree

☐ Strongly disagree

10. I would rather attend a fire than give a fire safety talk to a group of school children.

☐ Strongly agree

☐ Agree

☐ Neither agree or disagree

☐ Disagree

☐ Strongly disagree

11. I don't let things get on top of me.

☐ Strongly agree

☐ Agree

☐ Neither agree or disagree

☐ Disagree

☐ Strongly disagree

12. Being organised is not important to me.

☐ Strongly agree

☐ Agree

☐ Neither agree or disagree

☐ Disagree

☐ Strongly disagree

13. Accepting constructive criticism from others is not my strong point.

☐ Strongly agree

☐ Agree

☐ Neither agree or disagree

☐ Disagree

☐ Strongly disagree

14. Firefighting is a man's job.

☐ Strongly agree

☐ Agree

☐ Neither agree or disagree

☐ Disagree

☐ Strongly disagree

15. There should be more men in the Fire Service than women.

☐ Strongly agree

☐ Agree

☐ Neither agree or disagree

☐ Disagree

☐ Strongly disagree

16. It is acceptable to use strong language in the workplace.

☐ Strongly agree

☐ Agree

☐ Neither agree or disagree

☐ Disagree

☐ Strongly disagree

17. I do not have to be checked constantly when carrying out my work.

☐ Strongly agree

☐ Agree

☐ Neither agree or disagree

☐ Disagree

☐ Strongly disagree

18. I do not enjoy helping people.

☐ Strongly agree

☐ Agree

☐ Neither agree or disagree

☐ Disagree

☐ Strongly disagree

19. I find it hard to keep motivated to keep fit.

☐ Strongly agree

☐ Agree

☐ Neither agree or disagree

☐ Disagree

☐ Strongly disagree

20. I would not have a problem working with people from different groups, religious beliefs or backgrounds.

☐ Strongly agree

☐ Agree

☐ Neither agree or disagree

☐ Disagree

☐ Strongly disagree

21. I do not like to keep busy during the working day.

☐ Strongly agree

☐ Agree

☐ Neither agree or disagree

☐ Disagree

☐ Strongly disagree

22. It is not important to carry out tasks to a high standard.

☐ Strongly agree

☐ Agree

☐ Neither agree or disagree

☐ Disagree

☐ Strongly disagree

23. Health and safety regulation has made us a 'nanny state'.

☐ Strongly agree

☐ Agree

☐ Neither agree or disagree

☐ Disagree

☐ Strongly disagree

24. I would not take feedback during an appraisal well.

☐ Strongly agree

☐ Agree

☐ Neither agree or disagree

☐ Disagree

☐ Strongly disagree

25. If someone was horrible to me at work, I would try to avoid working with them.

☐ Strongly agree

☐ Agree

☐ Neither agree or disagree

☐ Disagree

☐ Strongly disagree

26. I do not enjoy fitness.

☐ Strongly agree

☐ Agree

☐ Neither agree or disagree

☐ Disagree

☐ Strongly disagree

27. I like to see people achieve their goals and aspirations.

☐ Strongly agree

☐ Agree

☐ Neither agree or disagree

☐ Disagree

☐ Strongly disagree

28. Fitting a smoke alarm is not as important as putting out a fire.

☐ Strongly agree

☐ Agree

☐ Neither agree or disagree

☐ Disagree

☐ Strongly disagree

29. I am always the first to volunteer for unpopular tasks.

☐ Strongly agree

☐ Agree

☐ Neither agree or disagree

☐ Disagree

☐ Strongly disagree

30. Jokes and banter are part and parcel of Fire Service life.

☐ Strongly agree

☐ Agree

☐ Neither agree or disagree

☐ Disagree

☐ Strongly disagree

31. I would not promote Fire Service values to a new member of the watch.

☐ Strongly agree

☐ Agree

☐ Neither agree or disagree

☐ Disagree

☐ Strongly disagree

32. Knowing your local community is just as important as knowing your firefighting equipment.

☐ Strongly agree

☐ Agree

☐ Neither agree or disagree

☐ Disagree

☐ Strongly disagree

33. I would tell a lie if it meant I could gain an advantage.

☐ Strongly agree

☐ Agree

☐ Neither agree or disagree

☐ Disagree

☐ Strongly disagree

34. There is no room for bullying in the workplace.

☐ Strongly agree

☐ Agree

☐ Neither agree or disagree

☐ Disagree

☐ Strongly disagree

35. I tend to find faults in other people.

☐ Strongly agree

☐ Agree

☐ Neither agree or disagree

☐ Disagree

☐ Strongly disagree

36. I am the kind of person who will not persevere until the task is complete.

☐ Strongly agree

☐ Agree

☐ Neither agree or disagree

☐ Disagree

☐ Strongly disagree

37. I do not remain calm in stressful situations.

☐ Strongly agree

☐ Agree

☐ Neither agree or disagree

☐ Disagree

☐ Strongly disagree

38. I like to work with other people.

☐ Strongly agree

☐ Agree

☐ Neither agree or disagree

☐ Disagree

☐ Strongly disagree

39. I have never told a lie in my life.

☐ Strongly agree

☐ Agree

☐ Neither agree or disagree

☐ Disagree

☐ Strongly disagree

40. I would challenge people in a constructive manner, if it meant I could achieve a more constructive outcome.

☐ Strongly agree

☐ Agree

☐ Neither agree or disagree

☐ Disagree

☐ Strongly disagree

41. I'd rather work with men than women.

☐ Strongly agree

☐ Agree

☐ Neither agree or disagree

☐ Disagree

☐ Strongly disagree

42. Firefighting first, fire prevention second.

☐ Strongly agree

☐ Agree

☐ Neither agree or disagree

☐ Disagree

☐ Strongly disagree

43. Creating fire safety leaflets in Braille is a waste of time.

☐ Strongly agree

☐ Agree

☐ Neither agree or disagree

☐ Disagree

☐ Strongly disagree

44. I'd rather be in the gym than listen to a Fire Service lecture.

☐ Strongly agree

☐ Agree

☐ Neither agree or disagree

☐ Disagree

☐ Strongly disagree

45. I am not a confident person.

☐ Strongly agree

☐ Agree

☐ Neither agree or disagree

☐ Disagree

☐ Strongly disagree

46. On occasions I can be lazy.

☐ Strongly agree

☐ Agree

☐ Neither agree or disagree

☐ Disagree

☐ Strongly disagree

47. The Fire Service should not employ disabled people in wheelchairs.

☐ Strongly agree

☐ Agree

☐ Neither agree or disagree

☐ Disagree

☐ Strongly disagree

48. If a female firefighter is too short to reach the ladder on the back of the fire engine, they shouldn't be in the job.

☐ Strongly agree

☐ Agree

☐ Neither agree or disagree

☐ Disagree

☐ Strongly disagree

49. I don't like monotonous tasks.

☐ Strongly agree

☐ Agree

☐ Neither agree or disagree

☐ Disagree

☐ Strongly disagree

50. I would not always support change.

☐ Strongly agree

☐ Agree

☐ Neither agree or disagree

☐ Disagree

☐ Strongly disagree

Now that you have completed the questionnaire, take the time to read through my own personal responses. Remember, there are no right or wrong answers to these questions. However, I have provided you with an explanation to each question as to why I have responded in this manner.

Personality Questionnaire Test – Richard's Responses

1. I tend to embrace change at work.

Strongly agree

Change in any organisation is important. I personally strongly believe that supporting change is essential to the role of a firefighter.

2. I would take just as much care and attention when mopping the fire station floor as I would when servicing my breathing apparatus set.

Agree

During your Fire Service career, you will mop the floor many, many times. It is important that you take just as much care with the menial tasks, as you do with the tasks that you enjoy. Personally, I used to really enjoy mopping the fire station floor!

3. I believe it is acceptable for people to get angry every now and again.

Disagree

Anger is an unpleasant emotion that can cause problems in a work setting. I agree that people need to get out their frustrations, but this can be done in other ways, such as in the gym, going running, or carrying out a favourite pastime. I play the drums in a band and this is a great way of de-stressing.

4. Different cultures of people in the community are not beneficial to society.

Strongly disagree

Respect for race and diversity is very important to your role as a firefighter. Why? Because you will be serving people in your community who are from different backgrounds and cultures. Society would be a very boring place if it was made up of people who were all the same. To put it another way, imagine if you could only choose one type of car, including one type of colour! Diversity is a wonderful thing – learn to embrace it.

5. If I witnessed a work colleague being bullied by another employee I would leave them both to sort it out themselves. Getting involved would probably make it worse.

Strongly disagree

Any behaviour that is inappropriate should be challenged immediately.

This does not mean you should become aggressive or confrontational, but instead you should challenge any form of bullying or harassment as it is not tolerated in the Fire Service.

6. If I made a mistake I would own up to it straight away.

Agree

Honesty and integrity in the Fire Service are important. Your work colleagues will want to be able to trust you. After all, their life could be in your hands one day.

"Is honest when working with others and accepts accountability for own actions" forms part of the PQAs. Remember what I wrote earlier – read, learn and understand the PQAs and you will find the questionnaire far easier to understand.

7. I have been known on occasions to panic and lose control.

Disagree

When the Fire Service turn up to an incident, the waiting members of the public do not expect them to panic or lose control! Again, read the PQAs and you will gain a feel for the kind of response they are after.

8. With regards to change, I believe that you shouldn't fix things if they are not broken.

Strongly disagree

If we go back to question number 1, you will see that this question is very similar, albeit it is posed in a different manner. Remember to make your responses consistent.

9. I find it easy to concentrate on tasks, despite external distractions.

Agree

Firefighters must be capable of carrying out many different tasks whilst under pressure. That pressure may come in the form of external engine noise from the fire engine, the heat from the fire or even screaming members of the public. Whatever happens, you must remain calm at all times and concentrate on the task in hand.

10. I would rather attend a fire than give a fire safety talk to a group of school children.

Disagree

Now if we are totally honest with ourselves, who wouldn't enjoy tackling a fire in a burning building? I used to love it! Providing nobody was trapped or became injured, this is exactly what I joined for. However, the modern-day Fire Service has changed, and so have the people who are part of it. If you want to be a firefighter, then you will have to get used to enjoying fire safety. It is true that a firefighter can save more lives through preventative work, than putting out fires.

11. I don't let things get on top of me.

Agree

Being a firefighter can sometimes be a stressful occupation. Therefore, it is important that you remain calm and keep your emotions in check.

12. Being organised is not important to me.

Strongly disagree

If a firefighter is not organised, then he or she will not be able to carry out their job properly. I have never heard of a firefighter who is late for work, forgets to bring their fire kit to work or does not clean their equipment. Being organised is all part and parcel of the firefighter's role.

13. Accepting constructive criticism from others is not my strong point.

Disagree

During your career you will receive many appraisals from your line manager. You must be able to take constructive feedback positively, simply because it will help you to improve. Commitment to development is an important PQA – read it.

14. Firefighting is a man's job.

Strongly disagree

When I joined the Fire Service in 1993, there were very few female firefighters – to me this was wrong. Women are just as capable as men when it comes to fighting fires. In fact, I would go as far as saying that the majority of women I worked with in the Fire Service were better than most of the men!

15. There should be more men in the Fire Service than women.

Strongly disagree

See my answer to question 14.

16. It is acceptable to use strong language in the workplace.

Strongly disagree

Swearing, and or abusive language, does not promote the right type of image for an organisation such as the Fire Service. When you join the service, you will be expected to act as a role model – and that means not only the way you look and act, but also the way you talk.

17. I do not have to be checked constantly when carrying out my work.

Agree

If you read the PQAs, it will state that firefighters should be capable of completing work as instructed without being checked constantly.

18. I do not enjoy helping people.

Disagree

Firefighters by their very nature enjoy helping people and caring for their local community. If you do not enjoy helping people, this is not the job for you!

19. I find it hard to keep motivated to keep fit.

Disagree

As you will be fully aware, you need to be fit in order to become a firefighter. You will find then when you eventually join the service; it will be your responsibility to maintain your levels of fitness.

20. I would not have a problem working with people from different groups, religious beliefs or backgrounds.

Strongly agree

See my response to question 4.

21. I do not like to keep busy during the working day.

Disagree

Firefighters are active people. If you are not attending fires, or giving community safety talks, then you should be reading your operational procedures, training, or checking over your equipment.

22. It is not important to carry out tasks to a high standard.

Disagree

Simply read the PQA 'Commitment to excellence'! There is no room for poor standards in the Fire Service. Your life, and the lives of your work colleagues and the members of public whom you serve, rely on you to carry out your work to a high standard.

23. Health and safety regulation has made us a 'nanny state'.

Strongly disagree

Whilst there are many people out there who believe health and safety has gone too far, it has in fact saved many thousands of lives. Health and safety, and also risk assessment, are two very important elements of the firefighter's role.

24. I would not take feedback well during an appraisal.

Disagree

See my response to question 13.

25. If someone was horrible to me at work, I would try to avoid working with them.

Disagree

There will be times when you don't get on with people in the Fire Service. Whilst you should not accept any form of bullying or harassment, you should make every effort to get along with everyone at work. After all, your life could depend on theirs, and vice-versa.

26. I do not enjoy fitness.

Disagree

See my previous answers to questions of this nature.

27. I like to see people achieve their goals and aspirations.

Agree

If you read the PQA of commitment to development, you will read something along the following lines:

"Actively encourages and supports others to improve their proficiency".

28. Fitting a smoke alarm is not as important as putting out a fire.

Disagree

Community fire safety is just as important, if not more important, than fighting fires. Remember, you can save far more lives through preventative work than you can fighting fires.

29. I am always the first to volunteer for unpopular tasks.

Agree

There will be many unpopular tasks to carry out in the Fire Service. Be one of those people who volunteers!

30. Jokes and banter are part and parcel of Fire Service life.

™ Strongly disagree

Now I am not saying you shouldn't have fun at work, far from it. What I am saying is there is no room for bullying or harassment at work. Being the butt of jokes continuously can be an unpleasant experience – I've seen it happen.

31. I would not promote Fire Service values to a new member of the watch.

Disagree

The values of the Fire Service are what it stands for. All new members of the watch should be encouraged to learn them and apply them.

32. Knowing your local community is just as important as knowing your firefighting equipment.

Agree

As a firefighter you will be serving your local community. Therefore, it makes perfect sense that you know just as much about your local community as you do about your equipment.

33. I would tell a lie if it meant I could gain an advantage.

Strongly disagree

As previously stated, there is no room for dishonesty in the Fire Service.

34. There is no room for bullying in the workplace.

Strongly agree

Hopefully you are starting to get the picture!

35. I tend to find faults in other people.

Disagree

Someone whom continually finds faults in others can be unpleasant to work with. Yes, it is important that we take on-board constructive criticism, but nobody likes a 'know it all'. Learn to work with your colleagues and embrace each other's differences.

36. I am the kind of person who will not persevere until the task is complete.

Disagree

Firefighters sometimes have to persevere in order to complete a task. This is especially the case during difficult road traffic collisions where a casualty is badly trapped inside the vehicle. Sometimes it will take hours to extricate a casualty. Whatever happens, you always persevere.

37. I do not remain calm in stressful situations.

Disagree

As I have previously stated, firefighters must remain calm and in control at all times, regardless of the pressures involved.

38. I like to work with other people.

Agree

One of the PQAs involves 'working with others'. As I am sure you are aware, working as part of a team is all part and parcel of Fire Service life. If you cannot work as part of a team, don't join!

39. I have never told a lie in my life.

Disagree

Now this is a tricky one! Anyone who 'agrees' is more than likely not being honest. After all, we have all told a white lie at some point in our lives! This question is designed to assess your level of honesty. I have told a few small white lies at some point in my life, therefore I am going to be honest when responding to the statement.

40. I would challenge people in a constructive manner, if it meant I could achieve a more constructive outcome.

Agree

Being able to challenge people in a constructive way demonstrates a level of confidence, especially if the result achieves a positive outcome. Read the PQAs and somewhere you will find a statement that is relevant to challenging in a constructive manner.

41. I'd rather work with men than women.

Strongly disagree

If you do not like working with a particular sex, don't apply!

42. Firefighting first, fire prevention second.

Disagree

As I have previously stated, a firefighter can save more lives through education and preventative work. Whilst fighting fires is very important, the first step is to educate the public in an attempt to prevent them from happening in the first place.

43. Creating fire safety leaflets in Braille is a waste of time.

Strongly disagree

Just because a person is visually impaired, it does not mean they should receive a lower level of service from their firefighters than anyone else. Many Fire Services now print fire safety leaflets in Braille and also in different languages.

44. I'd rather be in the gym than listen to a Fire Service lecture.

Disagree

Listening to Fire Service lectures and presentations are just as important as going to the gym!

45. I am not a confident person.

Disagree

Simply read the PQA that is relevant to confidence and resilience.

46. On occasions I can be lazy.

Disagree

Firefighters are not lazy people. They are hardworking, caring, professional and conscientious.

47. The Fire Service should not employ disabled people in wheelchairs.

Strongly disagree

The Fire Service is an equal opportunities employer. Just because a person is disabled, or in a wheelchair, it does not mean they are incapable of working, in fact the exact opposite. There are many different roles

National Firefighter Questionnaire 137

in the Fire Service, such as call operators and administrative workers.

48. If a female firefighter is too short to reach the ladder on the back of the fire engine, they shouldn't be in the job.

Strongly disagree

Here's my view on this – if the firefighter cannot reach the ladder, then there is a problem with the fire engine, not the firefighter!

49. I don't like monotonous tasks.

Disagree

Remember how I said that I enjoyed mopping the fire station floor? Monotonous tasks are part and parcel of Fire Service life. What is important is that you carry out the task to the same standard, regardless of how many times you have to do it.

50. I would not always support change.

Strongly disagree

Simply go back to my previous comments regarding change and how important it is to the modern-day Fire Service.

Chapter 6
Verbal Reasoning Tests

Verbal Reasoning Test

More recently, some Fire and Rescue Services across the UK have chosen to implement other types of verbal reasoning tests to the National Firefighter Questionnaire. So, it is incredibly important that you check with your favoured Service to find out which tests you will be facing during their recruitment process.

So, you may not need to use this section at all! If you do though, see below for a sample verbal reasoning test which is more generic in its content than the National Firefighter Questionnaire. Read the instructions below before starting, and good luck!

During the test below, there are 10 practice passages which each contain 3 questions. Answer each question based solely on the information provided.

You must select either TRUE, FALSE or CANNOT SAY based on the information provided in the passage.

Further instructions:

- You have 10 minutes to complete the test.

- Concentrate fully on each test.

- Circle the answer you believe to be correct.

- If unsure of an answer you should select the one that you believe to be correct.

- Avoid all forms of wild guessing.

- Once you have completed the test check your answers with the ones that are provided.

Top Tip From Richard McMunn

Answer the questions based solely on the information provided Candidates who sit verbal reasoning tests often fall into the trap of answering the question based on fact, rather than answering the question based solely on the information provided in the text. I have already stated that the type of question you are likely to encounter will involve a passage of text followed by a series of questions which must be answered either TRUE, FALSE or CANNOT SAY based on the information given. Let me give you an example of how people fall foul of the CANNOT SAY option.

Read the following text before answering the question as either TRUE, FALSE or CANNOT SAY based on the information provided.

A uniform is a set of standard clothing worn by members of an organisation whilst participating in that organisation's activity. Modern uniforms are worn by armed forces and paramilitary organisations such as; police, emergency services and security guards, in some workplaces and schools and by inmates in prisons. In some countries, officials also wear uniforms in some of their duties; such is the case of the Commissioned Corps of the United States Public Health Service or the French Prefects.

Q. Police officers are required to wear a uniform.

The answer to the question is **CANNOT SAY** based on the information provided. Many candidates will answer this question as TRUE; simply because we all know that police officers do in fact wear a uniform. The important lesson here is to only answer the question based solely on the information provided, regardless of what you know to be fact.

QUESTION 1

Read the following text before answering the questions as either TRUE, FALSE or CANNOT SAY from the information given.

ANALYSTS PROVE FORECASTERS WRONG

The Office for National Statistics said internet shopping and sales of household goods had been better in October compared with previous months. However, sales of clothing and footwear, where many retailers cut prices before Christmas, were particularly weak.

The increase came as a surprise to many analysts who were predicting a 0.4% fall in internet shopping and sales of household goods. The rise meant that retail sales volumes in the three months to January were up by 2.6% on the previous quarter. The final quarter of the year is a better guide to the underlying trend than one month's figures.

Some analysts cautioned that the heavy seasonal adjustment of the raw spending figures at the turn of the year made interpreting the data difficult. Even so, the government will be relieved that spending appears to be holding up despite the squeeze on incomes caused by high inflation, rising unemployment, a weak housing market and the crisis in the eurozone.

Retail sales account for less than half of total consumer spending and do not include the purchase of cars or eating out. The ONS said that its measure of inflation in the high street – the annual retail sales deflator – fell to 2.2% last month, its lowest level since November 2009. Ministers are hoping that lower inflation will boost real income growth during the course of 2017.

A - TRUE	B - FALSE	C - CANNOT SAY
Circle A if the question is TRUE from the information provided	Circle B if the question is FALSE from the information provided	Circle C if you CANNOT SAY from the information provided.

1. Ministers hope that higher inflation will boost real income growth during 2012.

      A   **B**   **C**

2. Analysts predicted a 0.4% rise in the sales of household goods.

      A   **B**   **C**

3. The crisis in the eurozone is contributing to the squeeze on incomes.

      A   **B**   **C**

QUESTION 2

Read the following text before answering the questions as either TRUE, FALSE or CANNOT SAY from the information given.

LONG-SERVICE PAYMENTS

Employees who attain fifteen years' continuous service between 7th November 2016 and 30th June 2017 shall qualify for the long-service payment at the rate applicable at the time. Employees who are promoted to a higher role during this period will cease to qualify for the payment but will receive a minimum pay increase on promotion of £300 per annum, which will be achieved through partial protection of the long-service payment.

Where the pay assimilation process on 7th November 2016 created a basic pay increase of more than 7%, and the employee was in receipt of the long-service payment, the payment has been reduced with effect from that date by the amount that the increase exceeded 7%. The consequent pay rates were set out in circular NJC/01/16.

PAY PROTECTION FOR EMPLOYEES ON THE RETAINED DUTY SYSTEM

Where an employee on the retained duty system has not received a pay increase of at least 7% (for the same pattern and level of activity) following full implementation of the pay award effective from 7th November 2016, the fire and rescue authority may introduce arrangements to ensure that such an increase is achieved.

ACTING UP AND TEMPORARY PROMOTION

The NJC recognises that in the early stages of implementing the Integrated Personal Development System it may, on occasions, be difficult to apply the principles at Paragraph 19 of Section 4 Part B. Fire and rescue authorities, employees and trade unions should therefore adopt a co-operative and common-sense approach to any problems that might arise.

A - TRUE	B - FALSE	C - CANNOT SAY
Circle A if the question is TRUE from the information provided	Circle B if the question is FALSE from the information provided	Circle C if you CANNOT SAY from the information provided.

1. If an employee who is on the retained duty system has not received a pay increase of at least 7% following the introduction of the pay award, the fire and rescue service must introduce arrangements to ensure that such an increase is achieved.

    A   B   C

2. Employees who attain fifteen years' continuous service between 7th November 2015 and 30th June 2016 shall qualify for the long-service payment at the rate applicable at the time.

    A   B   C

3. The pay assimilation process on 7th November 2003 created a basic pay increase for all employees of more than 7%.

    A   B   C

QUESTION 3

Read the following text before answering the questions as either TRUE, FALSE or CANNOT SAY from the information given.

DATA WAREHOUSES

A data warehouse is the main source of information for an organisation's historical data. Its historical data is often referred to as its corporate memory. As an example of how a data warehouse can be put to good use, an organisation would use the information stored in its data warehouse to find out how many particular stock items they sold on a particular day in a particular year. They could also ascertain which employees were off sick on any given day or any given year. The data stored within the warehouse contains essential information so that managers can make appropriate management decisions.

A data warehouse is normally large in size as the information stored usually focuses on basic, structured and organised data. Some of the characteristics of the data in a data warehouse are as follows:

• Time-variant – changes to the data in the database are tracked and recorded so that reports can be produced showing changes over time;

• Non-volatile – the data in the database is never over-written or deleted but is retained for future reporting;

• Integrated – the database contains data from most or all of an organisation's operational applications and this data is useful and meaningful for further processing and analysis.

A - TRUE	B - FALSE	C - CANNOT SAY
Circle A if the question is TRUE from the information provided	Circle B if the question is FALSE from the information provided	Circle C if you CANNOT SAY from the information provided.

1.   Integrated and non-volatile data form some of the characteristics of a data warehouse.

            A   B   C

2.   It is not possible to identify which employees were on sick leave from the information stored in a data warehouse.

            A   B   C

3.   Corporate memory is an alternative name given to historical data.

            A   B   C

QUESTION 4

Read the following text before answering the questions as either TRUE, FALSE or CANNOT SAY from the information given.

THE IMPORTANCE OF HEALTH AND SAFETY IN THE WORKPLACE

You must protect the safety and health of everyone in your workplace, including people with disabilities, and provide welfare facilities for your employees.

Basic things you need to consider are outlined below.

WELFARE FACILITIES

For your employees' wellbeing you need to provide:

- Toilets and hand basins, with soap and towels or a hand-dryer; drinking water.
- A place to store clothing (and somewhere to change if special clothing is worn for work).
- Somewhere to rest and eat meals.

HEALTH ISSUES

To have a healthy working environment, make sure there is:

- Good ventilation – a supply of fresh, clean air drawn from outside or a ventilation system.
- A reasonable working temperature (usually at least 16°C, or 13°C for strenuous work, unless other laws require lower temperatures).
- Lighting suitable for the work being carried out.
- Enough room space and suitable workstations and seating.
- A clean workplace with appropriate waste containers.

SAFETY ISSUES

- To keep your workplace safe, you must:
- Properly maintain your premises and work equipment.
- Keep floors and traffic routes free from obstruction.
- Have windows that can be opened and also cleaned safely.
- Make sure that any transparent (eg glass) doors or walls are protected or made of safety material.

A - TRUE	B - FALSE	C - CANNOT SAY
Circle A if the question is TRUE from the information provided	Circle B if the question is FALSE from the information provided	Circle C if you CANNOT SAY from the information provided.

1. It is the responsibility of the employer for keeping a workplace safe.

   A   B   C

2. Providing the employee with a suitable workstation is a consideration for the employer when making the workplace safe.

   A   B   C

3. An employer must ensure that all floor surfaces are non-slip in order to prevent slips, trips, and falls.

   A   B   C

QUESTION 5

Read the following text before answering the questions as either TRUE, FALSE or CANNOT SAY from the information given.

MAGISTRATE TRAINING

The entire selection process for becoming a magistrate can take approximately 12 months, sometimes longer depending on the area.

Once you have been accepted you will be required to undertake a comprehensive training course which is usually held over a 3-day period (18 hours). During this course you will learn the necessary skills that are required in order to become a magistrate.

The training is normally carried out by the Justice Clerk who is responsible for the court. He/she will usually be the legal advisor during your magistrate sittings. They will help you to develop all the necessary skills required in order to carry out your duties professionally and competently.

You will carry out your training as part of a group with other people who have been recruited at the same time as you. This is extremely beneficial as it will allow you to learn in a safe environment.

Training will be given using a variety of methods, which may include pre-course reading, small-group work, use of case studies, computer-based training and CCTV. It is recognised that magistrates are volunteers and that their time is valuable, so every effort is made to provide all training at times and places convenient to trainees. The Ministry of Justice booklet 'Serving as a Magistrate' has more information about the magistracy and the role of magistrates, and is available to applicants.

A - TRUE	B - FALSE	C - CANNOT SAY
Circle A if the question is TRUE from the information provided	Circle B if the question is FALSE from the information provided	Circle C if you CANNOT SAY from the information provided.

1. The comprehensive training course for becoming a magistrate usually consists of 3 days which is divided into 6 hours of training per day.

A   B   C

2. An applicant can find out more about the role of a magistrate by reading the Ministry of Justice booklet 'Serving as a Magistrate'.

A   B   C

3. The selection process for becoming a magistrate will take no longer than 12 months.

A   B   C

QUESTION 6

Read the following text before answering the questions as either TRUE, FALSE or CANNOT SAY from the information given.

HOW TO ENROL IN OUR ONLINE SELLERS' PROGRAMME

To enrol in our online sellers' programme, you must have an email account, access to the Internet, have a UK distribution facility and also hold the full UK distribution rights to the item(s) you want to sell.

You must have a UK bank account capable of receiving payments via electronic bank transfer (BACS), as this is the only method of payment we offer. Each product you wish to sell in our programme must meet our minimum eligibility standards. These standards relate to quality, value, subject matter, production standards and compliance with intellectual property laws. We reserve the right to remove any products if they do not meet our standards. You are not permitted to sell any products that are deemed to be pornographic or racist.

Any books that you wish to sell via our sellers' programme must have a 10 or 13-digit ISBN number and applicable barcode printed on the back of the book in the bottom right-hand corner.

The barcode must scan to match the ISBN of the book. If the item you want to sell is a music CD then the CD must be in a protective case which meets the relevant British Standard.

The title and artist name must be printed on and readable from the spine (the thin side of the CD). Once again, the CD must contain a barcode which must scan to match the EAN or UPC.

If your item is a DVD or VHS video. Rules that apply to music CDs are also applicable to DVD products.

A - TRUE	B - FALSE	C - CANNOT SAY
Circle A if the question is TRUE from the information provided	Circle B if the question is FALSE from the information provided	Circle C if you CANNOT SAY from the information provided.

1. The barcode on a CD must be printed on the back in the bottom right-hand corner.

    A   B   C

2. Pornographic products are permitted in the online sellers' programme.

    A   B   C

3. ISBN is short for International Standard Book Number.

    A   B   C

QUESTION 7

Read the following text before answering the questions as either TRUE, FALSE or CANNOT SAY from the information given.

WHAT CRITERIA DO WE USE TO DECIDE IF TRADE DISTRIBUTION IS APPROPRIATE?

Firstly, we will only consider a distribution relationship with publishers who have a UK-based storage and representation arrangement. Generally, we will hold a larger stock than would normally be required of a wholesaler, but we do need to have easy access to top-up facilities within the UK.

In addition, it is imperative that the titles are represented to the trade in order to generate UK sales. Whether this is via a UK-based sales/ marketing presence, or one based overseas, is not important, as long as it is effective in selling the titles to the target audience. Although we offer some promotional assistance through our weekly/monthly publications we do not offer sales and marketing as a service per se.

MINIMUM TURNOVER/LINES

The publisher should normally be able to demonstrate a realistic expectation of turnover in excess of £50k per annum at RRP and have a minimum of 5 lines. However, these targets are both negotiable where appropriate.

WHAT TERMS WILL BE REQUIRED?

Final discount and credit terms will be agreed on a case-by-case basis. Stock will be held on a consignment basis and we will provide monthly statements of sales and other management information. Invoicing will be against sales achieved each month and within the credit terms agreed.

A - TRUE	B - FALSE	C - CANNOT SAY
Circle A if the question is TRUE from the information provided	Circle B if the question is FALSE from the information provided	Circle C if you CANNOT SAY from the information provided.

1. All invoices are paid 30 days in arrears.

      A   B   C

2. An application from a publisher with a turnover of £49k will not be accepted.

      A   B   C

3. Applicants who reside in the Republic of Ireland will not be considered for a trade account.

      A   B   C

QUESTION 8

Read the following text before answering the questions as either TRUE, FALSE or CANNOT SAY from the information given.

THE ROLE OF THE AMBULANCE SERVICE

Most people believe that the Ambulance Service is simply there to respond to emergency incidents such as road traffic collisions (RTCs), seriously ill or injured patients, fires and other such incidents. While these are the core roles that the service undertakes, there are also a number of other important duties that are carried out, such as patient transport services.

The latter is carried out by the employees of the Ambulance Service who carry disabled, elderly and vulnerable people to and from out-patient appointments, hospital admissions and also day centres and clinics.

Behind the operational ambulance crew is a team of people who have different roles, all designed to provide the necessary support required that is so valued by the community.

To begin with, there are the 999 call operators who take the initial calls. Their job is to gather as much information as possible about the emergency call, the nature of the incident, its location and the level of response that is required.

These people are integral to the Ambulance Service and are crucial to patient care. For example, if a patient is critically ill they may need to talk the caller through a life-saving procedure while they wait for the ambulance crews to get there.

A - TRUE	B - FALSE	C - CANNOT SAY
Circle A if the question is TRUE from the information provided	Circle B if the question is FALSE from the information provided	Circle C if you CANNOT SAY from the information provided.

1. The 999 call operators do not travel in the ambulance with the paramedics.

A   B   C

2. Responding to road traffic collisions forms part of the core role of the Ambulance Service.

A   B   C

3. 999 call operators may need to talk the caller through a life-saving procedure while they wait for the ambulance crews to get there.

A   B   C

QUESTION 9

Read the following text before answering the questions as either TRUE, FALSE or CANNOT SAY from the information given.

WHAT IS A CUSTOMER CHARTER?

A Customer Charter is a statement as to how a company will deliver a quality customer service. The main purpose of a Customer Charter is to inform customers of the standards of service to expect, what to do if something goes wrong and how to make a complaint. In addition to this a Customer Charter also helps employees by setting out clearly defined standards of how they should perform within the organisation in relation to customer service delivery.

IS IT NECESSARY FOR AN ORGANISATION TO HAVE ONE?

Whilst not a legal requirement, a Customer Charter is an ideal way of helping organisations define with their customers, and others, what that service should be and the standard that should be expected. The charter will also help customers get the most from an organisation's services, including how to make a complaint if they are dissatisfied with any aspect of service or if they have ideas for improvement.

OTHER POINTS TO CONSIDER

A Customer Charter should be written in a clear and user-friendly manner. In addition to this, a Crystal Mark endorsement by the Plain English Campaign would enhance its status. If appropriate, it should be displayed in a prominent place, so all customers can see it. The Customer Charter must be available in different formats, such as large print and audio, so that customers with particular needs can access it. If an organisation is part of an industry where a regulator has been appointed, details of how to contact the regulator should be included.

A - TRUE	B - FALSE	C - CANNOT SAY
Circle A if the question is TRUE from the information provided	Circle B if the question is FALSE from the information provided	Circle C if you CANNOT SAY from the information provided.

1. A Customer Charter is a legal requirement within an organisation.

A   B   C

2. A Customer Charter must be written using a Crystal Mark endorsement by the Plain English Campaign.

A   B   C

3. The Customer Charter may be available in different formats, such as large print and audio, so that customers with particular needs can access it.

A   B   C

QUESTION 10

Read the following text before answering the questions as either TRUE, FALSE or CANNOT SAY from the information given.

WHAT IS A BALANCE SHEET?

A balance sheet is a snapshot of a company's financial position at a particular point of time in contrast to an income statement, which measures income over a period of time.

A balance sheet is usually calculated for March 31, last day of the financial year. A financial year starts on April 1 and ends on March 31. For example, the period between April 1, 2016 and March 31, 2017 will complete a financial year. A balance sheet measures three kinds of variables: assets, liabilities and shareholder's equity.

Assets are things like factories and machinery that the company uses to create value for its customers. Liabilities are what the company owes to third parties (e.g. outstanding payments to suppliers). Equity is the money initially invested by shareholders plus the retained earnings over the years.

These three variables are linked by the relationship: Assets = Liabilities + Shareholder's equity. Both assets and liabilities are further classified based on their liquidity, that is, how easily they can be converted into cash.

Current liabilities are liabilities that are due within a year and include interest payments, dividend payments and accounts payable. Long-term assets include fixed assets like land and factories as well as intangible assets like goodwill and brands. Finally, long-term liabilities are basically debt with maturity of more than a year.

A - TRUE	B - FALSE	C - CANNOT SAY
Circle A if the question is TRUE from the information provided	Circle B if the question is FALSE from the information provided	Circle C if you CANNOT SAY from the information provided.

1. A financial year starts on March 31 and ends on April 1.

A   B   C

2. It can be said that the liquidity of both assets and liabilities is how easily they can be converted into cash.

A   B   C

3. A balance sheet is a legal requirement and every company must have one.

A   B   C

Now that you have reached the end of the test, check your answers with the ones that are provided in the next section.

Verbal Reasoning Test Answers and Explanations

QUESTION 1

1. Ministers hope that higher inflation will boost real income growth during 2012.

Answer: B.

Explanation: The sentence states that ministers hope that 'lower' inflation will boost real income growth, not higher. Therefore, the statement is false.

2. Analysts predicted a 0.4% rise in the sales of household goods.

Answer: B.

Explanation: The passage states that analysts were predicting a 0.4% fall in sales of household goods, not rise. Therefore, the statement is false.

3. The crisis in the eurozone is contributing to the squeeze on incomes.

Answer: A.

Explanation: This statement is true based on the information provided in the passage.

QUESTION 2

1. If an employee who is on the retained duty system has not received a pay increase of at least 7% following the introduction of the pay award, the fire and rescue service must introduce arrangements to ensure that such an increase is achieved.

Answer: B.

Explanation: This statement is false because the sentence states that the fire and rescue service 'may' introduce arrangements; it does not say they 'must'.

2. Employees who attain fifteen years' continuous service between 7th November 2015 and 30th June 2016 shall qualify for the long-service payment at the rate applicable at the time.

Answer: B.

Explanation: This statement is false because the passage states '7th November 2016' and '30th June 2017', not 2015 and 2016 as stated in the question.

3. The pay assimilation process on 7th November 2016 created a basic pay increase for all employees of more than 7%.

Answer: C.

Explanation: We cannot say if this statement is true or false. It does not guarantee that 'all' employees received a pay rise.

QUESTION 3

1. Integrated and non-volatile data form some of the characteristics of a data warehouse.

Answer: A

Explanation: It is true. These two characteristics are detailed in the list at the bottom of the passage.

2. It is not possible to identify which employees were on sick leave from the information stored in a data warehouse.

Answer: B

Explanation: It is possible to ascertain which employees were off sick from the information stored in a data warehouse. Therefore, the statement is false.

3. Corporate memory is an alternative name given to historical data.

Answer: A

Explanation: This is true according to the second sentence of the passage.

QUESTION 4

1. It is the responsibility of the employee for keeping a workplace safe.

Answer: C

Explanation: This passage seems to focus on what the employer must do to keep the workplace safe. It makes no mention of what the employee must do.

2. Providing the employee with a suitable workstation is a consideration for the employer when making the workplace safe.

Answer: A

Explanation: This is mentioned in the penultimate point of the section 'HEALTH ISSUES'. Therefore, the statement is true.

3. An employer must ensure that all floor surfaces are non-slip in order to prevent slips, trips, and falls.

Answer: C

Explanation: While this is often true in health and safety law, it is not mentioned in the passage. Therefore, we cannot say.

QUESTION 5

1. The comprehensive training course for becoming a magistrate usually consists of 3 days which is divided into 6 hours of training per day.

Answer: C.

Explanation: We are told in the second paragraph that the training usually held over a 3-day period, and consists of 18 hours. However, it does not say anywhere that this is evenly divided into 6 hours per day. Therefore, we cannot say.

2. An applicant can find out more about the role of a magistrate by reading the Ministry of Justice booklet 'Serving as a Magistrate'.

Answer: A.

Explanation: We know this to be true from the final sentence of the passage.

3. The selection process for becoming a magistrate will take no longer than 12 months.

Answer: B.

Explanation: We know this to be false from the first sentence of the passage.

QUESTION 6

1. The barcode on a CD must be printed on the back in the bottom right-hand corner.

Answer: C.

Explanation: The penultimate sentence of the passage highlights the need for CDs to have a barcode, but, unlike on books, there is no mention of whether it needs to be on the bottom right-hand corner or not. So, we cannot say.

2. Pornographic products are permitted in the online sellers' programme.

Answer: B.

Explanation: At the end of the second paragraph, the passage clearly states that pornographic products are not permitted. Therefore, the answer is false.

3. ISBN is short for International Standard Book Number.

Answer: C.

Explanation: This statement is true. However, the passage makes no reference to it. So, based on the information provided by the passage, the answer is cannot say.

QUESTION 7

1. All invoices are paid 30 days in arrears.

Answer: C.

Explanation: This is not made clear in any section of the passage. Therefore, we cannot say.

2. An application from a publisher with a turnover of £49k will not be accepted.

Answer: B.

Explanation: Although the penultimate paragraph makes reference to an expected turnover of £50k per annum, it also states that the targets are negotiable. Because the targets are negotiable, we cannot confirm whether the statement is true or false. As such, we must select cannot say as the correct answer.

3. Applicants who reside in the Republic of Ireland will not be considered for a trade account.

Answer: C

The passage states that they will only consider a distribution relationship with publishers who have a UK-based storage and representation arrangement. However, the statement doesn't make reference to applicants who 'reside' abroad, e.g. in the Republic of Ireland.

So, it is entirely plausible that there may be applicants who reside in the Republic of Ireland, and also have a UK-based storage and representation arrangement.

However, the answer is still C, because we cannot say with absolute certainty that someone residing in the Republic of Ireland will or will not be considered; there is more information we need than just their address.

QUESTION 8

1. The 999 call operators do not travel in the ambulance with the paramedics.

Answer: C.

Explanation: While we know that this realistically does not happen, the passage makes no specific reference to the contrary. Therefore, we cannot say.

2. Responding to road traffic collisions forms part of the core role of the Ambulance Service.

Answer: A.

Explanation: The first paragraph specifically confirms this statement.

3. 999 call operators may need to talk the caller through a life-saving procedure while they wait for the ambulance crews to get there.

Answer: A.

Explanation: The final paragraph mentions this word for word.

QUESTION 9

1. A Customer Charter is a legal requirement within an organisation.

Answer: B.

Explanation: Paragraph two clearly states that a Customer Charter is not a legal requirement. Therefore, the answer is false.

2. A Customer Charter must be written using a Crystal Mark endorsement by the Plain English Campaign.

Answer: B.

Explanation: Paragraph three states that a Customer Charter should be written in a clear and user-friendly manner. It states that a Crystal Mark endorsement by the Plain English Campaign would enhance its status. However, the use of a Crystal Mark is not compulsory. Therefore, the statement is false.

3. The Customer Charter may be available in different formats, such as large print and audio, so that customers with particular needs can access it.

Answer: B.

Explanation: The passage states that "The Customer Charter must be available...". The question is asking whether it 'may' be available. Therefore, the correct answer is false.

QUESTION 10

1. A financial year starts on March 31 and ends on April 1.

Answer: B.

Explanation: The second paragraph states that a financial year starts on April 1 and ends on March 31, not the other way around. Therefore, the correct answer is false.

2. It can be said that the liquidity of both assets and liabilities is how easily they can be converted into cash.

Answer: A.

Explanation: The fourth paragraph specifically confirms this. Therefore, the answer is true.

3. A balance sheet is a legal requirement and every company must have one.

Answer: C.

Explanation: The passage makes no reference to this statement. Therefore, cannot say is the correct answer.

Chapter 7
Mechanical
Reasoning Tests

Depending on the Fire and Rescue service you're applying to, you may face mechanical reasoning tests. Mechanical comprehension tests have been used to assess a candidate's ability to work with and understand mechanical concepts.

Many mechanical comprehension tests require you to concentrate on 'mechanical principles' rather than making calculations, and as such will include diagrams and pictures as part of the question.

For example, you may be shown a diagram of a series of cogs and be asked which way a specific cog is turning based on the rotation of an adjacent cog. Other questions may be concerned with 'mechanical advantage', or deal with simple pulley systems.

Either way, here are some tips on passing mechanical comprehension questions.

- The majority of employers will assess you on speed and accuracy. Therefore, you are advised against random 'guessing'. Over the years, it has become common practice for test-takers to wildly guess when taking tests that are multiple-choice in nature, especially towards the end of the test when they are running out of time.

- In order to stop this practice, more and more test administrators are deducting marks for incorrect answers. Therefore, during your preparation for your assessment we recommend you simply practice lots of test questions, but more importantly understand how the answer is reached.

- Whilst on the subject of multiple-choice questions, you will most probably find that there are more mechanical comprehension test questions than you can answer during the allocated time given for the test. If this is the case, do not worry. Many tests are designed so that you do not finish them. Once again, simply work as fast as you can but also aim for accuracy.

- If you come up against a difficult question during your mechanical comprehension test, move on, but remember to leave a gap on the answer sheet. If you fail to leave a gap, then each of the preceding answers will be incorrect.

- In the build-up to the test, if you feel like you are struggling with basic mechanical concepts, then we recommend you study a car manual such as Haynes. This will give you an idea of how mechanical concepts work. You can obtain Haynes manuals at: www.haynes.co.uk.

It's now time for you to try out the sample tests below. Read the questions carefully, and the answers are provided at the end of the section.

Mechanical Comprehension Test

Question 1

If the wheel rotates anticlockwise, what will happen to X?

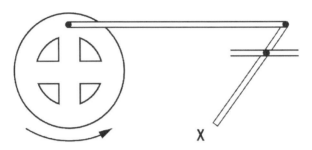

A. It will move to the right and stop.

B. It will move to the left and stop.

C. It will move left and right.

Question 2

Which chain will support the load on its own?

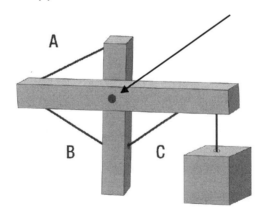

A	B	C	D
Chain A	Chain B	Chain C	None of them

Question 3

Which nail is likely to pull out first?

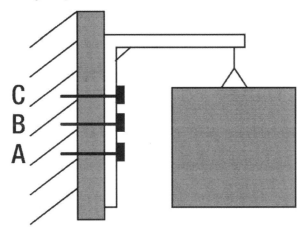

A	B	C	D
Nail A	Nail B	Nail C	All together

Question 4

If wheel A rotates anti-clockwise, which way, and how, will wheel B rotate?

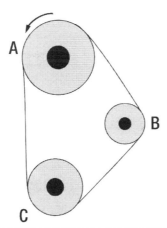

A	B	C	D
Clockwise / more rps	Clockwise / less rps	Anti-clockwise / more rps	Anti-clockwise / less rps

Question 5

Which way, and how, will cog C rotate?

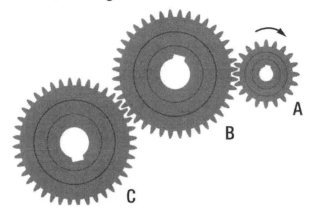

A	B	C	D
Clockwise / more rps than A	Clockwise / less rps than A	Anti-clockwise / more rps than A	Anti-clockwise / less rps than A

Question 6

Which lever will require more effort to lift the load?

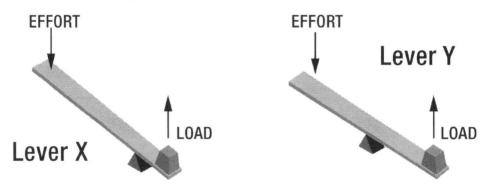

A	B	C
Lever X	Lever Y	Both the same

Question 7

How much force is required to lift the load?

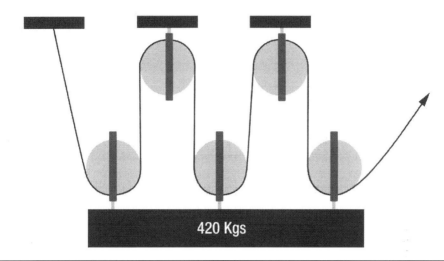

420 Kgs

A	B	C	D
140 kgs	210 kgs	90 kgs	70 kgs

Question 8

How much weight is required to hold the load?

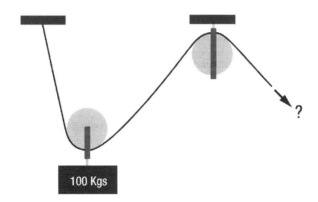

100 Kgs

A	B	C	D
400 kgs	200 kgs	100 kgs	50 kg

Question 9

If lever A moves in the direction shown, which way will B move?

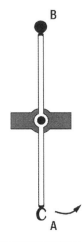

A	B	C	D
To the left	To the right	Backwards and forwards	It will not move

Question 10

If the motor wheel rotates in a clockwise direction, what happens to B and C?

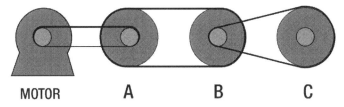

A. B and C will move clockwise.

B. B and C will move anti-clockwise.

C. B will move clockwise, and C will move anti-clockwise.

D. B will move anti-clockwise, and C will move clockwise.

Question 11

If weight is placed on the top of each stack of boxes, which stack would support the most weight?

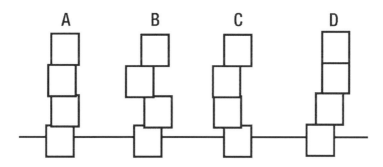

A	B	C	D
Stack A	Stack B	Stack C	Stack D

Question 12

If wheel A turns in an anti-clockwise direction, which way will wheel B turn?

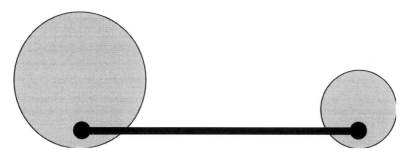

A	B	C	D
Clockwise	Anti-clockwise	Backwards and forwards	It won't move

Question 13

Which post is carrying the least heavy load?

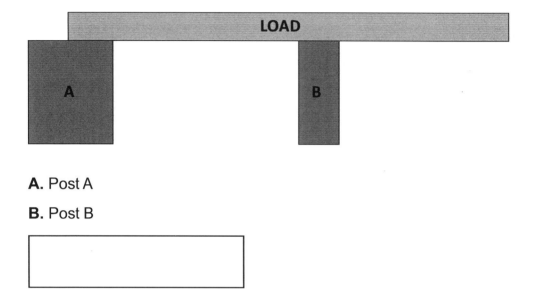

A. Post A

B. Post B

Question 14

Which pendulum will swing at the fastest swing rate?

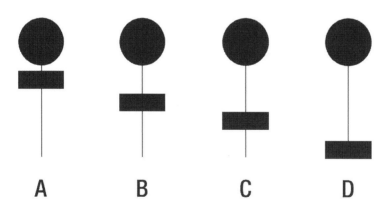

A	B	C	D
Pendulum A	Pendulum B	Pendulum C	Pendulum D

Question 15

If Cog B turns clockwise, which of the other cogs will also turn clockwise?

A	B	C	D
Cogs D and C	Cogs A, C and E	Cog D	Cogs D and E

Answers to Mechanical Comprehension Test

Q1. c

It will move left and right as the wheel rotates.

Q2. b

Chain B is the only one which can support the load independently.

Q3. c

Nail C is most likely to pull out first.

Q4. c

Wheel B will rotate anti-clockwise with more rps because it is smaller than the other two wheels.

Q5. b

Cog C will rotate clockwise with less rps than A because it has more teeth.

Q6. b

Lever Y will require more effort to lift the load because the fulcrum is further away from the load than lever X.

Q7. d

The load weighs 420 kgs and there are a total of six sections of rope supporting it. In order to calculate the force required to lift the load, simply divide the weight by the number of ropes in order to reach your answer:

- 420 ÷ 6 = 70 kg

Q8. d

In this scenario the weight is suspended by two pulleys. This means the weight is split equally between the two pulleys. If you want to hold the weight you only have to apply half the weight of the load, i.e. 100 ÷ 2 = 50 kgs.

Q9. a

B will move to the left in this situation.

Q10. a

B and C will move clockwise as the motor wheel moves clockwise.

Q11. a

Stack A is the most stable and will therefore support the most weight.

Q12. b

Because the two wheels are joined they will rotate the same way. If A rotates anticlockwise, wheel B will also.

Q13. a

Post A is carrying the least heavy load as the majority of force is placed on post B.

Q14. a

Pendulum A will swing the fastest speed rate. The lower down the weight, the slower the pendulum will swing.

Q15. c

Cog D is the only other cog which will rotate clockwise.

Chapter 8
A Few Final Words

You have now reached the end of the guide and I hope that you have found it a useful aid in your preparation for the firefighter selection process. No matter which Fire and Rescue Service in the country you wish to apply to,

Before I sign off, please take the time to read the following final pieces of advice that I have for you:

Carry out lots of practice.

Without practice you will not do yourself justice. As you already know, the selection process is extremely competitive, but don't let this put you off. The vast majority of candidates will be ill-prepared. Make sure you are 100% prepared!

Learn the PQAs.

Your life will be a lot easier if you read, learn and absorb the personal qualities and attributes that are relevant to the role. If you know them well, then many of the answers will jump out at you.

Be good with numbers.

You have to be competent in the use of numbers if you are to pass the written tests. Get yourself further practising aids from the website www.How2Become.com. Sign up for the online testing and also grab yourself a copy of our numerical reasoning testing books.

Never give in!

Perseverance is my favourite word. It has always served me well. Keep trying, not only in terms of applying to become a firefighter, but more importantly improving yourself. If you fail selection, find out why you have failed, and then go all out to improve in that area.

Finally, before you go to the interview, consider carrying out some volunteer work in your local community. I am aware that this will gain you higher marks during the interview!

Work hard, stay focused, and secure your dream career!

Richard McMunn

NEED A LITTLE EXTRA HELP WITH JOINING THE UK FIRE SERVICE?

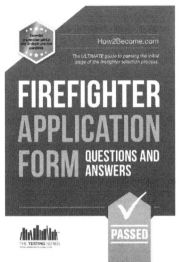 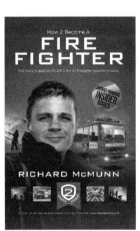 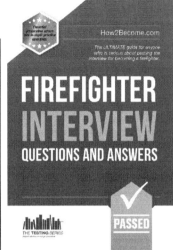

How2Become have created other FANTASTIC guides to help you prepare for the UK Firefighter selection process.

These exciting guides are filled with essential facts, to ensure that your preparation is thorough, and that you are completely ready for the process ahead. With our help, you can secure your dream career today.

FOR MORE INFORMATION ON OUR POLICE OFFICER GUIDES, PLEASE CHECK OUT THE FOLLOWING:
WWW.HOW2BECOME.COM

Printed in Great Britain
by Amazon